FEMINISM:
One Man's View

FEMINISM:
One Man's View

Alvin Plexico, PhD

High praise for
Feminism: One Man's View

"Many thanks to Alvin Plexico for his cogent insights into feminism. This book is a must-read for anyone who wants to understand what feminism is. His historical approach is a great way to understand feminism's impact."

**—Paula F. Casey, co-founder,
Tennessee Woman Suffrage Heritage Trail**

"Dr. Plexico is a guy who gets it! While his book is too sophisticated to be called a primer, it will be my twelve-year-old granddaughter's birthday present. He captures the components of feminism in logical order and presents them in an entertaining fashion."

—Jocelyn Dan Wurzburg, author of *Jocie: Southern Jewish American Princess and Civil Rights Activist*
The Tennessee Human Rights Commission established the Jocelyn Dan Wurzburg Civil Rights Award in her honor.

Library of Congress

ISBN: 978-1-7361525-3-9

Printed and bound in the United States of America
by Ingram Lightning Source

Cover design by Jacque Hillman

Editing, layout, and design: Jacque Hillman, Kim Stewart,
Jason Tippitt, and Katie Gould

The HillHelen Group LLC
www.hillhelengrouppublishers.com
hillhelengroup@gmail.com

This book is dedicated to the grandchildren my two daughters will raise. May they live in a time when people genuinely recognize and fully appreciate the important role that feminism can play in making the world a better place for all.

All proceeds from *Feminism: One Man's View*
will benefit the Tennessee Woman Suffrage Heritage Trail.
For more information about the trail, go to
https://tnwomansuffrageheritagetrail.com.

Table of Contents

Introduction

What images come to mind when you hear someone described as a feminist?

Ladies burning bras? Women walking topless in public? Millions of women marching in protest while wearing pink pussy hats?

Perhaps you might picture pioneer suffragists like Susan B. Anthony, Carrie Chapman Catt, Elizabeth Cady Stanton, Sojourner Truth, or others who fought in the struggle to secure the right for women to vote.

What comes to mind when you hear the word feminism?

The concept tends to generate a visceral response, either in favor or against. It can be so controversial partly because there's no agreed-upon definition for feminism. Politicians, news media, and others often use the word to incite an emotional response.

We rarely stop to think about what it means to be a feminist, or more importantly, what a pro-feminist approach could mean for women (and men).

Here are some definitions for feminism:

• Organized activity on behalf of women's rights and interests (Merriam-Webster Dictionary).

• The advocacy of women's rights on the grounds of equality of the sexes (Oxford Dictionary).

• A range of political movements, ideologies, and social movements that share a common goal: to define, establish, and achieve political, economic, personal, and social equality of sexes (*What Is Feminism?* by Chris Beasley).

I once saw a woman wearing a shirt with another definition: "Feminism is the radical notion that women are people."

I consider myself a feminist because I believe that women should receive equal pay, an equal voice, and absolute veto authority over issues that primarily affect their own health and well-being.

I don't claim to know everything there is to know about feminism. In fact, I have enough intellectual humility to understand that I know very little about feminism. As a man, I will never fully appreciate what it's like to be a woman, nor will I ever fully understand what feminism is or what it can become.

I do know that, as a lifelong learner, I'm open to other opinions—especially those that differ from my own.

If you're reading this book to get expert insights, I'm afraid you'll be disappointed. I am no expert. I am just one man with one opinion about often-misunderstood views of feminism.

Feel free to join the discussion at OneMansFeminism.org.

*"The enemy of feminism isn't men.
It's patriarchy, and patriarchy is not men.
It is a system, and women can support
the system of patriarchy just as men
can support the fight for gender equality."*

Justine Musk, Canadian author

Photo from US Department of State

In 2016, many Americans assumed Hillary Clinton would become the first female president of the United States. Her loss on Election Day took supporters by surprise. It also led to much soul-searching and analysis on subtle and overt prejudices against women who are competing in the male-dominated political arena.

1

Women in Politics

"**D**ad! What's happening?"

My youngest daughter texted me on election night 2016 when Florida appeared to be trending in favor of Donald Trump.

"Don't worry," I replied. "It's early."

Many Americans assumed that Hillary Clinton would be the first female president, especially when the alternative was a thrice-married philanderer who bragged about sexually assaulting women.

Here is how some prominent Republicans described then-candidate Trump:

• Colin Powell, former secretary of state and former chairman of the Joint Chiefs of Staff: In personal emails, widely reported after hackers leaked them in 2016, Powell described Trump as a "national disgrace" and "an international pariah." He also criticized Trump for adding fuel to the debunked, "racist" birther movement that sought to show that former President Barack Obama was born in another country. Powell wasn't particularly generous in his description of Clinton, either. In a

2014 email, Powell disparaged candidate Clinton as "greedy, not transformational," with "unbridled ambition."

• Barbara Bush, the former first lady: "I mean, unbelievable. I don't know how women can vote for someone who said what he said about Megyn Kelly; it's terrible."[1]

Bush was likely referring to Trump's criticism of Kelly, who moderated a debate in which she asked pointed questions on Trump's comments about women.

• Mitt Romney, former governor and 2012 Republican Party presidential nominee: "I wanted my grandkids to see that I simply couldn't ignore what Mr. Trump was saying and doing, which revealed a character and temperament unfit for the leader of the free world."[2]

As a military veteran with more than twenty-two years of service, I don't make assertions based solely on what others say about Donald Trump, but rather what he has said and done himself.

I served four commanders-in-chief during my service from 1990 to 2013. While I may have disagreed with them on policy issues, I never doubted their loyalty to our nation.

"Dad! How can this be happening?" This time, my daughter called when it looked as though Clinton would lose. Clinton fell short in the Electoral College, with only 232 votes to Trump's 306. She did win the popular vote, with the tally at 65,853,514 to 62,984,828 (48.18% to 46.09%).[3]

---

1. Sarah Friedmann, "These Barbara Bush Quotes About Trump Are Still So Relevant for American Women," *Bustle*, April 17, 2018, https://www.bustle.com/p/these-barbara-bush-quotes-about-trump-are-still-so-relevant-for-american-women-8823104

2. David A. Graham, "Which Republicans Oppose Trump?," *The Atlantic*, November 6, 2016, https://www.theatlantic.com/politics/archive/2016/11/where-republicans-stand-on-donald-trump-a-cheat-sheet/481449/

3. Federal Election Commission, https://www.fec.gov/resources/cms-content/documents/federalelections2016.pdf

"Sometimes, the election doesn't turn out the way you want," I said to my daughter. "I remember when Bill Clinton won re-election in 1996, even though I voted against him. I also voted for his opponent in 1992, but Clinton won anyway. He's just one person, and there are lots of checks and balances in our government to prevent one person, even the president, from causing too much damage."

I voted against Bill Clinton because I didn't believe he had the moral authority to lead our nation. If politicians cannot keep a promise to a spouse, I doubt they'll keep promises to me as a citizen.

Does this seem old-fashioned or judgmental?

As a husband of more than thirty years, I appreciate the importance of keeping one's promises—especially those made to a person with whom you join in "one union till death do you part." As a military veteran, I take seriously the oath I swore to "protect and defend."

And as a Christian, I believe in grace; however, this requires admitting sin and seeking forgiveness.

All right, enough preaching. Let's move on to what we can learn about feminism from the 2016 election, and what we can learn about elections that followed.

"Why were Trump's supporters so convinced that Clinton was the more corrupt candidate even as reporters uncovered far more damning evidence about Trump's foundation than they did about Clinton's?" Peter Beinart, a professor at City University of New York, asked in an interesting article for *The Atlantic* in August 2018.

Beinart answered his own question: "Likely because Clinton's candidacy threatened traditional gender roles. For many Americans, female ambition—especially in service of a feminist agenda—in and of itself represents a form of corruption."[4]

---

4. Peter Beinart, "What Trump Supporters Think of Corruption," *The Atlantic*, August 2018, https://www.theatlantic.com/politics/archive/2018/08/what-trumps-supporters-think-of-corruption/568147/

Beinart's observations helped me better understand how another group—evangelicals—voted in large numbers for Trump.

"While earlier in the campaign some pundits and others questioned whether the thrice-married Trump would earn the bulk of white evangelical support, fully eight-in-ten self-identified white, born-again/evangelical Christians say they voted for Trump, while just 16% voted for Clinton," according to Pew Research.[5]

This finding hit close to home because I identified as a born-again evangelical Christian, and I'm white. Notice, I used the past tense of "identified." Based on these findings, I no longer refer to myself as an evangelical.

As a Christian, it's difficult to support a leader without any regard for how his sins affect others or without any apparent understanding of repentance.

The last thing I want is for someone to associate my Christianity as support for the person who received a vast majority of the white, evangelical support. I still consider myself a Christian, but I can choose how to use my faith to help others and to share how my faith is open to all people.

I still puzzle over how many of my fellow Christians can put aside their claims to be the keepers of morality in leadership by supporting a person who, by his own admission, acts in immoral ways that are antithetical to an honest review of the Bible and teachings of Jesus Christ.

In his book *Believe Me,* author John Fea puts it this way: ". . . value voters still had to come to grips with an inconvenient truth: Trump appeared to be the most immoral candidate in recent memory. . . . His entire career, and his success as a television star and public figure, was built on vices incompatible with the moral

5. Jessica Martínez and Gregory A. Smith, "How the Faithful Voted: A Preliminary 2016 Analysis," Pew Research Center, November 9, 2016, http://www.pewresearch.org/fact-tank/2016/11/09/how-the-faithful-voted-a-preliminary-2016-analysis/

teachings of Christianity. And, by his own admission, he never, ever, asked forgiveness of his sins."[6]

Fea also describes how Christians, or values voters, overcame cognitive dissonance. "For too long, white Evangelical Christians have engaged in public life through a strategy defined by the politics of fear, the pursuit of worldly power, and a nostalgic longing for a national past that may have never existed in the first place."[7]

I can attest to hearing sermons about fear, power, and nostalgia. Not only was it a frequent message on Sunday morning, I also heard and engaged in similar discussions with fellow Christians.

"Fear never leads to peace. Fear never leads to joy. It always leads to anger, usually anger at those who are not like you," Fea goes on to explain.[8]

Beinart based his assertion on a 2010 study by Yale researchers Victoria Brescoll and Tyler Okimoto. They found that when female politicians were described as power-seeking, participants felt moral outrage—contempt, anger, or disgust.

"Voters are less likely to vote for female politicians when they perceive them as power-seeking, though male politicians are not penalized," Brescoll and Okimoto write. "Both a power-seeking image and expressed power-seeking intent can bias voters against female politicians."[9]

Why is there a double standard for female politicians?

I suspect it has a lot to do with our patriarchal society, with male domination that stretches back millennia.

---

6. John Fea, *Believe Me: The Evangelical Road to Donald Trump*, (Grand Rapids: Eerdmans, 2018).

7. Fea, *Believe Me*.

8. Fea, *Believe Me*.

9. Tyler G. Okimoto and Victoria L. Brescoll, "The Price of Power: Power Seeking and Backlash Against Female Politicians," *Personality and Social Psychology Bulletin*, 36(7), 923-936.

Interestingly, part of the 2010 Yale study was confirmed in 2018 research: "While the much-discussed 'gender gap' was the largest ever in 2016, it was only modestly greater than in 2012." Many women, researchers write, feel "trepidation towards the loss of 'traditional American family values,' including the preservation of separate spheres for men and women."[10]

This research ties together the religious angle of female politician animus and the reason why most white evangelicals, and most white women, voted for Donald Trump.

I hear the fear and frustration from my evangelical friends and family members. They pine for the days of yesteryear when American values were respected.

What they don't say, or perhaps what they don't fully appreciate, is that the "good ol' days" were not very good for a lot of people —including women.

Many of those who want to "make America great again" fail to describe exactly what that greatness would look like, or how that return to another time would impact those who have gained rights and status over the past many decades.

This lack of knowledge about historical context is supported by data describing how education played a role in the 2016 election.

"College-educated whites were more supportive of Clinton than they had been of Obama in 2012, while whites without a college degree moved even more dramatically toward Trump," the study says. Some of the statements used for the study included "women are too easily offended" and "women seek to gain power by getting control over men."

"Moving from one end of the sexism scale to the other was associated with more than a 30-point increase in support for Trump among the average likely voter," the authors noted. "Resentment

---

10. Diana C. Mutz, "Status Threat, Not Economic Hardship, Explains the 2016 Presidential Vote," *Proceedings of the National Academy of Sciences*, 115 (19).

over the changing racial make-up of the nation, and unease with the shifting role of women, played a much bigger role in his victory."[11]

Hillary Clinton acknowledged this fear of change during a 2017 presentation at the Professional Business Women of California Conference in San Francisco. "In this election (2016), there was a very real struggle between what is viewed as change that is welcomed and exciting to so many Americans, and change that is worrisome and threatening to so many others. And you layer that on the first woman president over that, and I think some people, women included, had real problems."[12]

Clinton is also quoted as saying, "There cannot be true democracy unless women's voices are heard. There cannot be true democracy unless women are given the opportunity to take responsibility for their own lives. There cannot be true democracy unless all citizens are able to participate fully in the lives of their country."

When asked in a 2017 article to provide one word to describe feminism, Clinton said, "Equality. And I will say: Feminism is the belief that men and women should be equal under the law, and in the economy, in our society. Not better. Not worse. Equal. And what I hope is that we will continue to move toward equality, because it still is the unfinished business in our country. And that's equality not only between men and women, but between races and ethnicities and all the divides that we are still struggling with."[13]

During the California business conference, Clinton also offered this advice: "As I think about all the activism we're seeing, in spite

11. Tom Jacobs, "More Evidence That Racism and Sexism Were Key to Trump's Victory," *Pacific Standard*, April 4, 2018.

12. Nicole Sazegar, "6 Hillary Clinton Quotes to Empower Women in the Workplace," *Entity*, September 7, 2017.

13. Lindsay Miller, "Hillary Clinton's One-Word Definition of Feminism Pretty Much Nails It," Popsugar, December 16, 2017, https://www.popsugar.com/news/Hillary-Clinton-Feminism-Quotes-Girls-Build-LA-2017-44369800

of all the noise and the nonsense, four words keep coming back at me: resist, insist, persist, enlist."

As you reflect on these four words, what do they mean to you? More importantly, how could you put these four words into action?

"The more we support women, the more we support democracy."
Hillary Clinton

* * *

Learning from the 2016 election is helpful, but what other lessons can be learned in more recent political races?

Let's start with some of the results from the 2018 midterm elections. The 116th Congress was the most diverse in US history, with 126 women, including 43 women of color. Unfortunately, the balance of diversity was not evident across party lines. There were 36 new women in the House after the 2018 midterm election, 35 of whom were Democrats. In the new House, 90% of the Republicans were white men while 38% of Democrats were white men.[14]

"The congressional freshman class of 2019 is perhaps best described in superlatives. It is the most racially diverse and most female group of representatives ever elected to the House, whose history spans more than 200 years. Women led the way to victory for House Democrats. They won more than 60% of the seats that Democrats flipped in what some termed the 'Year of the Woman,'" the *New York Times* reported in a November 11, 2018, article.[15]

The House would continue to include a majority of men; however, the nearly forty women elected to Congress reminded many of the twenty-four women elected in the last "Year of the Woman" in 1992.

---

14. Elise Viebeck, "Diversity on Stark Display as House's Incoming Freshmen Gather in Washington," *Washington Post*, November 13, 2018.

15. Catie Edmondson and Jasmine C. Lee, "Meet the New Freshmen in Congress," *New York Times*, January 3, 2019.

FEMINISM: One Man's View

One major distinction between 2018 and 1992 is that only one in ten House members were female after the 1992 election, compared with a House that was one in four female after the 2018 election.[16]

"In the 2018 elections, women played a bigger role than they have in any other election in American history," Elaine Karmack, a senior fellow at the Brookings Institute, wrote in a 2018 report.

"Two hundred and fifty-five women ran for office in the two major parties. Previous groundbreaking years for women were 1984, when Geraldine Ferraro ran as the first ever female vice-presidential nominee on Walter Mondale's ticket and, of course, 2016, when Hillary Clinton became the first woman presidential nominee of a national party," Karmack wrote. "But 2018 shares the most in common with 1992, when eleven women ran as major party candidates for the Senate and five were elected, and 106 women ran for the House, with 23 percent winning."[17]

While election results serve as one measure of political progress, what changes can be expected in terms of policies?

"Women are more likely to introduce bills of importance to families," Swanee Hunt and Andrea Dew Steele, who founded networks that foster women in public policy, wrote in a commentary for CNN. "They are much stronger advocates for women's health concerns, such as affordable contraception, breast cancer research, and domestic violence laws . . . Congresswomen, more than their male colleagues, champion family-friendly policies, including increasing the minimum wage, closing the wage gap, fighting for paid leave, expanding childcare options and improving education."[18]

---

16. Mary Jordan, "It's a Sea Change: CIA Agent, Nuclear Engineer, Flight Attendant Among the Record Number of Women Headed to Congress," *Washington Post*, November 9, 2018.

17. Elaine Kamarck, "2018: Another Year of the Woman," Brookings, November 7, 2018.

18. Swanee Hunt and Andrea Dew Steele, "A Seismic Shift in Government Is Coming and Here's Who Will Drive It," CNN, April 21, 2018.

How will the movement change Washington? Time will tell. "But outside the Beltway, a transformation has already begun," *Time* reported in 2018.

"In dozens of interviews with *Time*, progressive women described undergoing a metamorphosis. In 2016, they were ordinary voters. In 2017, they became activists, spurred by the bitter defeat of the first major female presidential candidate at the hands of a self-described 'pussy grabber.' Now, in 2018, these doctors and mothers and teachers and executives are jumping into the arena and bringing new energy to a Democratic Party sorely in need of fresh faces. About four times as many Democratic women are running for House seats as Republican women, according to the Center for American Women and Politics; in the Senate, the ratio is 2 to 1."[19]

Women's election success extended beyond the Beltway with more than 2,000 women serving in state legislatures in 2019, compared to 1,875 women in state legislatures prior to the 2018 elections, according to the Center for American Women and Politics at Rutgers University.[20]

Of note, when the Nevada legislature opened in 2019, it was the first time a state legislature included an overall female majority. A decade earlier, New Hampshire had a female majority in the state Senate in 2009-2010. Women made up 28.6% of all state legislators in 2019 compared with 24.3% in 2009—another example of progress made, but much more work to be done.[21]

While writing this book at what some may call the 2020

---

19. Charlotte Alter, "A Year Ago, They Marched. Now a Record Number of Women Are Running for Office," *Time*, January 18, 2018.

20. Alexi McCammond, "Why 2020 Could Be Different for Women," Axios, January 4, 2019.

21. Michelle L. Price, "Nevada Becomes 1st US State with Female-Majority Legislature," Associated Press, December 18, 2018.

campaign preseason, it was unclear how the Year of the Woman would influence the chances of a future female presidential candidate; however, it is noteworthy that the Democratic Party had six females contending at the beginning of the race.

"I don't think we appreciate how deeply set our expectations of how women are meant to behave are set. As much progress as women have made, we're pushing against all of human history here. It's still a pretty radical thing for a woman to seek to be president of the United States," Jennifer Palmieri, Clinton's former communications director and White House communications director under Obama, said in a 2019 interview.

"The expectations are just so much higher in terms of what the public wants from a woman," said Adrienne Elrod, former director of strategic communications for Clinton's campaign in 2016. "They want someone warm, friendly, grandmother-like, and also a hard-charger who can go into a meeting with ten male foreign leaders and crush the meeting. They want someone who has it all."[22]

The impact that women could have in future elections is phenomenal, when one considers that more women are registered to vote than men and that women vote in higher numbers than men. There's also been a gender gap in every midterm election since 2006 and every presidential election since 1980. This gap continues to widen, with Democrats' lead among women growing to 20 percentage points on average during the 2018 midterm elections.[23]

---

22. Alexi McCammond, "2018 Midterm Election Sets Record for Women in Congress," Axios, November 7, 2018.

23. Hayley Miller, "Women Are Placing Their 'I Voted' Stickers on Susan B. Anthony's Grave," Huffpost, November 6, 2018.

Dr. Christine Blasey Ford gives an oath before testifying before the Senate Judiciary Committee on September 27, 2018.

Brett Kavanaugh's nomination to the Supreme Court became a rallying cry and turning point for the Me Too movement after Dr. Christine Blasey Ford accused him of sexually assaulting her when she was a teenager.

2

#MeToo

While I was conducting research for this book, Dr. Christine Blasey Ford's allegation upended the hearing for then-Supreme Court Justice nominee Brett Kavanaugh.

Ford described in painful detail how she was sexually assaulted at a party she attended in 1982, when she was in high school. She said that she believed with 100 percent certainty that her attacker was Brett Kavanaugh. Following her testimony before the Senate Judiciary Committee on September 27, 2018, Kavanaugh swore before the same committee that he had never committed sexual assault. He forcefully denied Ford's allegations, along with those from other women who had come forward after Ford's claims.

What followed from the hearing was a classic Rorschach test, where what one saw was greatly influenced by what one already believed. For those who supported Kavanaugh's appointment to the Supreme Court, Ford must have been mistaken. For those opposed to his nomination, Kavanaugh was another example of how a powerful man could get away with sexual assault.

In the divided and highly charged political environment, many chose to use the moment to further their own agenda. Since I try to be objective as a researcher and writer, I reviewed social and traditional media from many different angles.

Here are examples of what was posted through social media:

Donald J. Trump, on Twitter:
@realDonaldTrump: Judge Kavanaugh showed America exactly why I nominated him. His testimony was powerful, honest, and riveting. . . .

Senator Mitch McConnell, on Twitter:
@senatemajldr: Democrats' mishandling of Dr. Ford's letter opened the floodgates for a deluge of uncorroborated, unbelievable mud from others. . . .

Ann Coulter, on Twitter:
@AnnCoulter: Dr. Ford had months to prepare—and then used her "fear of flying" to delay the hearing by a week. . . .

Kyle Griffin, on Twitter:
@kylegriffin1: Honesty of Dr. Ford and Kavanaugh: Dr. Ford is honest 59%. Kavanaugh is honest 46%.

US Senate photo

Senator Dianne Feinstein, press release:
Then Senator Dianne Feinstein released a statement reading: "At no point did I or anyone on my staff divulge Dr. Blasey Ford's name to press. She knows that and believes it, for which I'm grateful."

Senator Bob Casey, philly.com:
Casey wrote an opinion piece titled "Why I Believe Dr. Ford."

Senator Elizabeth Warren, on Twitter, shared this message and a video on the topic:

@ewarren: "Brett Kavanaugh was allowed to be angry. Dr. Ford wasn't. Women grow up hearing that being angry makes us unattractive. Well, today, I'm angry—and I own it."

US Senate photo

Lisa Boothe, on Twitter:

@LisaMarieBoothe: "Can everyone please stop pretending like Dr. Ford is credible now? She is NOT credible. It's painfully obvious. I feel like I've been living in the Twilight Zone."

Dan Rather, on Twitter:

@DanRather: "Imagine if this happened to your son or grandson," say many Kavanaugh defenders. As one blessed with both, I would respectfully counter that it is in the brave testimony of Christine Blasey Ford and other survivors that men can find the lessons for a more just future."

Art: Wanda Stanfill

Here are some headlines from media coverage:

• **CNN:** "Trump says it's 'a very scary time for young men in America.'"

• **Fox News:** "After Kavanaugh-Ford hearing, does MeToo face a backlash?"

• **PBS NewsHour:** "Ford testified. Kavanaugh testified. What did we learn?"

• **Reuters:** "With anger and tears, Kavanaugh denies sex assault allegation."

• **Yahoo News:** "During Christine Blasey Ford's testimony, contempt for women was on full display."

• **NewsCenterMaine.com:** "1600 men say they believe Christine Blasey Ford in a full-page newspaper ad."

Generally, I try to watch major press conferences live. I prefer to get first-hand information along with applicable context, rather than rely solely on what's reported through the media.

During President Trump's September 26 press conference, the afternoon before the Ford/Kavanaugh Senate hearing, a reporter asked what message Trump was sending to young men.

His response reveals a lot about Trump's views, but it also reveals a lot about how others may view the subject of sexual assault. Here is the press conference transcript:[24]

"I think it's a great question. This is a very big moment for our country, because you have a man who's very outstanding, but he's got very strong charges against him, probably charges that nobody's going to be able, to be—to prove.

"So I could have you chosen for a position—I could have you, or you, or you, anybody—and somebody could say thing (ph)—and it's happened to me, many times, where false statements are made. And honestly, nobody knows who to believe. I could pick another Supreme Court judge—justice. I could pick another one, another one, another one—this could go on forever. Somebody could come and say thirty years ago, twenty-five years ago, ten years ago, five years ago, he did a horrible thing to me. He did this, he did that, he did that and, honestly, it's a very dangerous period in our country. And it's being perpetuated by some very evil people—some of them are Democrats, I must say—because some of them know that this is just a game that they're playing. It's a con game. It's at the highest level. We're talking about the United States Supreme Court.

"This can go on forever. I can pick five other people. At a certain point, the people are going to say 'no, thank you.' This is the most coveted job, probably in the world.

---

24. White House press conference transcript, September 27, 2018, retrieved on June 5, 2019, https://www.whitehouse.gov/briefings-statements/press-conference-president-trump-2/

"And you know what? I would honestly say—because I interviewed great people for this job—he's great, but I interviewed other great people for this job.

"I could conceivably imagine going to one of them and saying it's too bad what happened to this wonderful man, but I'm going to choose you, number two. I want you to go. And I could conceivably be turned down by somebody that desperately wanted this job two months ago. . . .

"I heard you're innocent until proven guilty. I've heard this for so long and it's such a beautiful phrase. In this case, you're guilty until proven innocent. I think that is a very, very dangerous standard for our country."

These responses are told from the perspective of someone accused of sexual assault or falsely accused in his and his supporters' eyes. It's also told from the perspective of a president frustrated with the challenge to his authority in nominating a Supreme Court justice, perhaps concerned about future potential nominees turning down the opportunity to serve.

If I were to follow Trump's advice on what message we should send young men, I guess I would be sharing that "this" could happen to them. "This" is not sexual assault; "this" is being falsely accused of sexual assault.

I do not have a son, but if I did, I would hope the message that I would share with him is to always, *always*, treat women with dignity and respect. To be careful about making short-term choices that have long-term consequences. If a woman confides in you that she is a victim of sexual assault, believe her. Offer your sympathies, yes, but also offer to help get her the support to deal with this crisis.

There is a legal fund in which lawyers help sexual harassment victims who can't afford to pursue their cases, according to an Associated Press report. "In its early phases, the #MeToo movement was epitomized by professional women from the worlds of movie-making, media and politics who spoke out about sexual harassment. One year after its birth, as the movement remains vibrant, there are ever-growing resources to help financially struggling women, including many from low-wage workplaces, litigate their complaints."[25]

The week before the Senate hearings, Trump tweeted, "I have no doubt that, if the attack on Dr. Ford was as bad as she says, charges would have been immediately filed with local law enforcement authorities by either her or her loving parents. I ask that she bring those filings forward so that we can learn date, time, and place!"

During her opening statement before the Senate Judiciary Committee, Ford explained why she did not report her assault. "For a very long time, I was too afraid and ashamed to tell anyone the details. I did not want to tell my parents that I, at age fifteen, was in a house without any parents present, drinking beer with boys. I tried to convince myself that because Brett did not rape me, I should be able to move on and just pretend that it had never happened."[26]

This explanation is consistent with research that shows that 63% of sexual assaults are not reported to the police.[27]

Research also shows that the incidence of false reports is less than 10%. This means that when we hear a report of sexual assault, we can be more than 90% certain it happened, and we should be 100% empathetic to the courage it takes for a person to come forward about such a traumatic experience.[28]

---

25. David Crary, "Financially Hard-Up Women Get Help in Pursuing MeToo Cases," Associated Press, October 4, 2018.

26. Senate Judiciary Committee, September 26, 2018, written testimony of Dr. Christine Blasey Ford, https://www.judiciary.senate.gov/imo/media/doc/09-27-18%20Ford%20Testimony.pdf

27. Callie Marie Rennison, "Rape and Sexual Assault: Reporting to Police and Medical Attention," US Department of Justice, Office of Justice Programs, Bureau of Justice Statistics (2002), https://www.bjs.gov/content/pub/pdf/rsarp00.pdf

28. David Lisak, et al., "False Allegations of Sexual Assault: An Analysis of Ten Years of Reported Cases," *Violence Against Women*, 16, 1318-1334.

The week after the trial, on October 2, Trump said, "It is a very scary time for young men in America, where you can be guilty of something you may not be guilty of."

I use Trump as an example, but he's not alone when it comes to people, especially men, who fail to understand what it must be like to suffer a sexual assault.

A striking example of the different ways men and women view this issue comes from Dr. Jackson Katz, who shares this exercise:[29]

"I draw a line down the middle of a chalkboard, sketching a male symbol on one side and a female symbol on the other. Then I ask just the men: What steps do you guys take, on a daily basis, to prevent yourselves from being sexually assaulted? At first there is a kind of awkward silence as the men try to figure out if they've been asked a trick question. The silence gives way to a smattering of nervous laughter. Occasionally, a young guy will raise his hand and say, 'I stay out of prison.' This is typically followed by another moment of laughter, before someone finally raises his hand and soberly states, 'Nothing. I don't think about it.'

"Then I ask the women the same question. What steps do you take on a daily basis to prevent yourselves from being sexually assaulted? Women throughout the audience immediately start raising their hands.

"As the men sit in stunned silence, the women recount safety precautions they take as part of their daily routine: Hold my keys as a potential weapon. Look in the back seat of the car before getting in. Carry a cell phone. Don't go jogging at night. Lock all the windows when I sleep, even on hot summer nights. Be careful not to drink too much. Don't put my drink down and come back to it; make sure I see it being poured. Own a big dog. Carry Mace or pepper spray. Have an unlisted phone number. Have a man's voice

---

29. Jackson Katz, *The Macho Paradox: Why Some Men Hurt Women and How All Men Can Help* (Naperville, IL: Sourcebooks, 2006).

on my answering machine. Park in well-lit areas. Don't use parking garages. Don't get on elevators with only one man, or with a group of men. Vary my route home from work. Watch what I wear. Don't use highway rest areas. Use a home alarm system. Don't wear headphones when jogging. Avoid forests or wooded areas, even in the daytime. Don't take a first-floor apartment. Go out in groups. Own a firearm. Meet men on first dates in public places. Make sure to have a car or cab fare. Don't make eye contact with men on the street. Make assertive eye contact with men on the street."

I will never understand what it's like to be a woman who must constantly be on guard against, or to have suffered from, sexual assault. This means that I have an additional responsibility to keep my mouth closed and my mind open to issues related to it.

* * *

What follows is a brief history of the #MeToo movement.

The hashtag gained prominence in 2017 following the allegations of sexual harassment against movie producer Harvey Weinstein; however, the movement has roots dating back to 2006.

Tarana Burke founded the #MeToo movement to help survivors of sexual violence, particularly young women of color from low-wealth communities, find pathways to healing. Using the idea of "empowerment through empathy," the movement was ultimately created to ensure survivors know they're not alone in their journey.[30]

"The 'me too' movement has built a community of survivors from all walks of life," the Me Too website says. "By bringing vital conversations about sexual violence into the mainstream, we're helping to destigmatize survivors by highlighting the breadth and impact sexual violence has on thousands of women, and we're helping those who need it to find entry points to healing. Ultimately, with survivors at the forefront of this movement, we're

---

30. Me Too, https://metoomvmt.org.

aiding the fight to end sexual violence. We want to uplift radical community healing as a social justice issue and are committed to disrupting all systems that allow sexual violence to flourish." [31]

One resource is the Time's Up Legal Defense Fund, administered by the National Women's Law Center. NWLC President Fatima Goss Graves said, "We've helped people bring cases they could not have brought otherwise. People know they have a place to turn to. We can make it a reality that no matter where you work, you can work safely and with dignity." [32]

It's impossible to know where the #MeToo movement will lead us over the coming months and years, but one thing is clear: We are never going back to the days when treating women disrespectfully, and largely getting away with it, is the norm for our society.

There will be pain, and there will be many more powerful (and not-so-powerful) men who will be held accountable for their actions. This is a good thing in the end. Change is hard, but change we must for the sake of future generations of women and the men who must respect them.

31. Me Too, https://metoomvmt.org.

32. Crary, 2018.

Our Roll of Honor

Containing all the
Signatures to the "Declaration of Sentiments"
Set Forth by the First

Woman's Rights Convention,

held at
Seneca Falls, New York
July 19-20, 1848

LADIES:

Lucretia Mott
Harriet Cady Eaton
Margaret Pryor
Elizabeth Cady Stanton
Eunice Newton Foote
Mary Ann M'Clintock
Margaret Schooley
Martha C. Wright
Jane C. Hunt
Amy Post
Catherine F. Stebbins
Mary Ann Frink
Lydia Mount
Delia Mathews
Catherine C. Paine
Elizabeth W. M'Clintock
Malvina Seymour
Phebe Mosher
Catherine Shaw
Deborah Scott
Sarah Hallowell
Mary M'Clintock
Mary Gilbert

Sophronia Taylor
Cynthia Davis
Hannah Plant
Lucy Jones
Sarah Whitney
Mary H. Hallowell
Elizabeth Conklin
Sally Pitcher
Mary Conklin
Susan Quinn
Mary S. Mirror
Phebe King
Julia Ann Drake
Charlotte Woodward
Martha Underhill
Dorothy Mathews
Eunice Barker
Sarah R. Woods
Lydia Gild
Sarah Hoffman
Elizabeth Leslie
Martha Ridley

Rachel D. Bonnel
Betsey Tewksbury
Rhoda Palmer
Margaret Jenkins
Cynthia Fuller
Mary Martin
P. A. Culvert
Susan R. Doty
Rebecca Race
Sarah A. Mosher
Mary E. Vail
Lucy Spalding
Lovina Latham
Sarah Smith
Eliza Martin
Maria E. Wilbur
Elizabeth D. Smith
Caroline Barker
Ann Porter
Experience Gibbs
Antoinette E. Segur
Hannah J. Latham
Sarah Sisson

GENTLEMEN:

Richard P. Hunt
Samuel D. Tillman
Justin Williams
Elisha Foote
Frederick Douglass
Henry W. Seymour
Henry Seymour
David Spalding
William G. Barker
Elias J. Doty
John Jones

William S. Dell
James Mott
William Burroughs
Robert Smallbridge
Jacob Mathews
Charles L. Hoskins
Thomas M'Clintock
Saron Phillips
Jacob P. Chamberlain
Jonathan Metcalf

Nathan J. Milliken
S. E. Woodworth
Edward F. Underhill
George W. Pryor
Joel Bunker
Isaac VanTassel
Thomas Dell
E. W. Capron
Stephen Shear
Henry Hatley
Azaliah Schooley

3

History of Feminism

I love history, because understanding where we have been can help guide us to a better place. History also provides context for current events and issues driving the social agenda.

"Feminism" was Merriam-Webster's word of the year in 2017.

So, what's the history of feminism?

Plato favored "the total political and sexual equality of women, advocating that they be members of his highest class," according to the Columbia Encyclopedia.

It seems strange (and a little sad) that we're debating women's equality 2,400 years since Plato first argued for women's rights. It seems even stranger to think about how little progress has been made, even in places like America, where freedom is supposedly written into our DNA.

Of course, many could argue that the freedoms guaranteed by our forefathers were enjoyed primarily by wealthy white men. It took a civil war and a civil rights movement before Blacks earned the freedoms that many took for granted then and still do. We have a long way to go before *all* Americans enjoy equality as it should be, and hopefully someday will be. This includes the rights of women, which is where feminism plays a role in our nation's history. It can be seen in the eighteenth century, which is sometimes referred to as the Age of Enlightenment.

Mary Wollstonecraft, often considered to be one of the first feminist philosophers, wrote *A Vindication of the Rights of Women* in 1792. According to Margaret Walters, Wollstonecraft's work provides a foundation for feminist thought.[33]

Interestingly, Wollstonecraft wrote about a belief that inequality was the fault of both men and women, and she described how education could provide a basis for change. She refused to accept the expected role of women in society, arguing for a feminist equality.

The notion that men and women are both responsible for inequality supports findings of modern researchers, who describe both genders sharing a fear of losing traditional values and roles. The role of education in creating change remains to be seen, especially when one considers that many don't recognize that there's a problem that requires any change.

* * *

Some scholars offer three historical phases to describe feminism, with a different area of focus for each:
• Legal equality (nineteenth and early twentieth centuries).
• Cultural equality (1960s–1980s).
• A third wave of activities from the 1990s through today.

Legal equality
An example of a nineteenth century feminist would be Florence Nightingale, credited as the mother of modern nursing. Less well known was her work in social reform, including efforts to allow

---

33. Margaret Walters, *Feminism: A Very Short Introduction*, October 27, 2005, Oxford University Press.

female participation in the workforce. She shared a belief that women had the same potential as men but did not enjoy the same opportunities. Sadly, these same arguments are made today.[34]

Another leader of feminist thought in the nineteenth century was Harriet Martineau, who wrote an article titled "Female Industry," which appeared in the *Edinburgh Journal* in 1859. She argued that education and employment were both important tenets of any reform efforts; however, she did not join her fellow feminists in calling for a woman's right to vote.[35]

During the abolitionist movement of the nineteenth century, women at times were not allowed to speak at anti-slavery conventions. This naturally led some women to argue for increased freedoms for themselves while arguing for the freedom of slaves.

Male leaders of the first World Anti-Slavery Convention in 1840 ignored two feminists, Elizabeth Cady Stanton and Lucretia Mott. Eight years later, the two women organized a women's rights convention in Seneca Falls, New York. There, participants drafted a declaration of independence for women.

In 1850, feminists Sojourner Truth, Abby Kelley Foster, and others spoke at the first National Women's Rights Convention. In the audience was Susan B. Anthony, one of our nation's most recognized feminists. One year later, in Akron, Ohio, Sojourner Truth delivered a speech titled "Ain't I a Woman?" Truth's words still are recited today as a call for women's rights.[36]

Feminism was a "household term in the United States by

---

34. Mark Bostridge, *Florence Nightingale: The Making of an Icon*, Farrar, Straus, and Giroux, popular image described, p. 251.

35. Harriet Martineau, *Harriet Martineau's Autobiography*, 1877, Cambridge University Press, pp. 79–80.

36. Library of Congress, The Learning Page, Lesson Two: Changing Methods and Reforms of the Woman's Suffrage Movement, 1840-1920, "The first convention ever called to discuss the civil and political rights of women . . . (excerpt)," retrieved on April 24, 2019.

1913," according to Nancy F. Cott. In the following decades, many feminist issues would be discussed in the public square, including the original Equal Rights Amendment written by Alice Paul and Crystal Eastman in 1921.[37]

Both World War I and World War II influenced the feminist movement, because women took over many work roles that men had traditionally filled before those men were called off to distant lands to fight. After the "War to End All Wars," most women returned to their domestic roles in the twenties and thirties before they were called to fill the gap again during the second world war.

This time, after peace treaties were signed, many women were not content to return to the house. Some pushed forward with changes in the workplace, although it would take decades of struggle—and changes in the law through many court cases—for these changes to become widespread.

In 1929, Virginia Woolf wrote an essay titled "A Room of One's Own," in which she argued against those who opposed rights for women, specifically those who chose to use the word "feminism" in a negative connotation. Woolf came to the defense of a fellow writer, Rebecca West, when she was attacked as a feminist. West replied, "I myself have never been able to find out precisely what feminism is: I only know that people call me a feminist whenever I express sentiments that differentiate me from a doormat, or a prostitute."[38]

In addition to supporting World War II in jobs symbolized by Rosie the Riveter, more than 300,000 women served in the American military as Women's Army Corps (WAC) and Women Accepted for Volunteer Emergency Service (WAVES) in the US Navy Reserve. After the war, many factories supporting combat

---

37. Nancy F. Cott, *The Grounding of Modern Feminism*, New Haven: Yale University Press, 1987.

38. Elyce Rae Helford, in Gary Westfahl, *The Greenwood Encyclopedia of Science Fiction and Fantasy*, Greenwood Press, 2005: 289-90.

munitions and machinery closed. Those that remained open laid off female employees to make room for veterans.

The United Nations played an important role in global feminism, establishing the Commission on the Status of Women in 1946 and issuing the Universal Declaration of Human Rights in 1948, which protects "the equal rights of men and women."[39]

Cultural and political equality

The period known as first-wave feminism slowly evolved into a second wave of feminism, which lasted from the 1960s through the 1980s and focused on cultural and political equality for women. Of particular interest to feminists during this time period was ending discrimination based on gender.

Women were enrolling in higher education in larger numbers by then and demanding equal access to jobs, sports, and social organizations. In 1972, Title IX of the Education Amendments began protecting people from "discrimination based on sex in education programs or activities that receive federal financial assistance." The text of Title IX reads: "No person in the United States shall, on the basis of sex, be excluded from participation in, be denied the benefits of, or be subjected to discrimination under any education program or activity receiving federal financial assistance."[40]

Like many laws regarding equal rights, it took a long time for the effects to be fully enforced. Some argue that the intent of the law is still not fully or equally enforced today.

During the so-called second wave of feminism, the term

---

39. United Nations, Short History of the Commission on the Status of Women, retrieved June 4, 2019, https://www.un.org/womenwatch/daw/CSW60YRS/CSWbriefhistory.pdf

40. US Department of Education, Title IX and Sex Discrimination, retrieved May 15, 2019, https://www2.ed.gov/about/offices/list/ocr/docs/tix_dis.html

"women's liberation" was first used in print in the US in 1966,[41] although there were instances of the phrase in France dating back to 1911. The term "liberation" has been used as part of the feminist movement as long as the movement has been around.[42]

Third wave

Beginning in the 1990s, a third wave of feminism rose out of what some believed was a failure of second-wave feminist efforts. Younger women wanted to continue the unfinished work of their mothers and grandmothers, to challenge some assumptions not only about gender roles but about gender itself. Efforts were also made to reach out to women of color and women in poorer communities, especially as it related to their participation in politics, such as voting and rallying in the public square.[43]

These efforts to reach out to women of color and women in poorer communities are captured in a social theory known as womanism. Alice Walker coined the term to describe the intersectionality of culture, class, and other lenses through which feminism can be viewed. Walker said, "Womanism is to feminism as purple is to lavender."[44]

The history of feminism is still being written, and it will take many brave women and men willing to challenge the status quo before feminism reaches its full potential to make the workplace a more equal place for all.

---

41. Kathie Sarachild, "Consciousness-Raising: A Radical Weapon," in K. Sarachild, C. Hanisch, F. Levine, B. Leon, and C. Price, (eds), *Feminist Revolution*, NY: Random House, 1978, pp. 144-50.

42. Estelle B. Freedman, *No Turning Back: The History of Feminism and the Future of Women*, London: Ballantine Books, 2003.

43. D'Ann Campbell, *Women at War with America: Private Lives in a Patriotic Era*, Harvard University Press, 1984.

44. Joy James, *The Black Feminist Reader*, Wiley-Blackwell, 2001.

Who's who among feminists

What follows is an incomplete list of notable feminists. Photos are from the Library of Congress unless otherwise indicated.

Jane Addams, 1860–1935

Known as the mother of social work. Earned the Nobel Peace Prize. Co-founded Hull House, where educated women taught poorer people. Lobbied for a juvenile court system and labor legislation for women. Founding member of the National Child Labor Committee. https://www.womenshistory.org/education-resources/biographies/jane-addams

Chimamanda Ngozi Adichie, 1977–

Nigerian novelist, writer of short stories and nonfiction, including *We Should All Be Feminists*. In 2008, she was awarded a MacArthur Genius Grant. https://www.chimamanda.com

Maya Angelou, 1928–2014

American poet, singer, memoirist, and civil rights activist. Best known for *I Know Why the Caged Bird Sings,* her first of seven autobiographies. She wrote three books of essays, several collections of poetry, and much more. Active in the civil rights movement. https://www.mayaangelou.com

Photo: Clinton Presidential Library

Susan B. Anthony, 1820–1906

American social reformer and women's rights activist who played a pivotal role in the woman suffrage movement. Called for the first Woman Suffrage Convention in Washington, DC, in 1869. Arrested for voting on November 18, 1872. In 1873, she was tried and fined one hundred dollars with costs after the judge ordered the jury to find her guilty. Anthony refused to pay but was not imprisoned and thus was unable to appeal the verdict. Established a press bureau in 1898 to feed articles on woman suffrage to the national and local press. In 1900, she pledged the cash value of her life insurance to meet the University of Rochester's financial demands for the admission of women. Met with President Theodore Roosevelt in 1905 about submitting a suffrage amendment to Congress. In 1906, she gave her "Failure Is Impossible" speech at her eighty-sixth birthday celebration. https://susanb.org/her-life

Alice Stone Blackwell, 1857–1950
Suffragist and editor of the leading American women's rights newspaper. https://www.britannica.com/biography/Alice-Stone-Blackwell

Elizabeth Blackwell, 1821–1910
The first woman in America to receive a medical degree. Championed the participation of women in the medical profession and ultimately opened her own medical college for women. https://www.womenshistory.org/education-resources/biographies/elizabeth-blackwell

Harriot Stanton Blatch, 1856–1940
Founded the Equality League of Self-Supporting Women. Director of Women's Land Army during World War I. Worked through the National Woman's Party for federal equal rights amendment. Assisted her mother, Elizabeth Cady Stanton, and Susan B. Anthony in completing the *History of Woman Suffrage*. https://www.britannica.com/biography/Harriot-Eaton-Stanton-Blatch

Josephine Elizabeth Butler, 1828–1906

English feminist and social reformer in the Victorian era. She campaigned for woman suffrage, the right of women to better education, the abolition of child prostitution, an end to human trafficking of young women and children into European prostitution, and the end of coverture in British law. (Coverture was a legal doctrine that gave married women no legal standing apart from their husbands.) http://www.gutenberg.org/ebooks/author/5456

Carrie Clinton Lane Chapman Catt, 1859–1947

Founded the League of Women Voters and the International Woman Suffrage Alliance. Directed the National American Woman Suffrage Association, 1915-1920. Devised the "Winning Plan," which coordinated state suffrage campaigns with the drive for a constitutional amendment—which helped ensure final victory. https://www.womenshistory.org/education-resources/biographies/carrie-chapman-catt

Shirley Chisholm, 1924–2005

First Black woman in Congress (1968). First woman and first Black person to seek the nomination for president of the United States from one of the two major political parties (1972). Chisholm's motto and the title of her autobiography—*Unbossed and Unbought*—illustrated her outspoken advocacy for women and for minorities during the seven terms that she served in the US House of Representatives. https://www.womenshistory.org/education-resources/biographies/shirley-chisholm

Hillary Rodham Clinton, 1947–

American politician and diplomat who served as the first lady of the United States from 1993 to 2001, senator from New York from 2001 to 2009, secretary of state from 2009 to 2013, and the Democratic Party's nominee for president in the 2016 election. https://www.hillaryclinton.com

Brittney Cooper, PhD, 1980–

Associate professor of women's and gender studies and Africana studies at Rutgers University. Co-founder of the popular Crunk Feminist Collective blog. Her cultural commentary has been featured on *MSNBC's All In With Chris Hayes, Melissa Harris-Perry,* Al Jazeera's *Third Rail,* the *New York Times,* the *Washington Post, NPR, PBS,* Ebony.com, Essence.com, TheRoot.com, and TED.com. http://www.brittneycooper.com/

Dorothy Cotton, 1930–2018

Leader in the civil rights movement as the Southern Christian Leadership Conference's education director. Recipient of the National Freedom Award from the National Civil Rights Museum in Memphis, Tennessee, in 2010. https://www. dorothycottoninstitute.org/about-dorothy-cotton/about-dorothy-cotton-biography/

 **Angela Yvonne Davis, 1944–**

American political activist, academic, and author. Prominent counterculture activist in the 1960s while working with the Communist Party USA, of which she was a member until 1991. Involved briefly in the Black Panther Party during the civil rights movement. Ran for US vice president on the unsuccessful Communist Party ticket in 1980. https://www.britannica.com/biography/Angela-Davis

Anne Dallas Dudley, 1876–1955

President of the Tennessee Equal Suffrage Association from 1915 to 1917, when she was elected third vice president of the National American Woman Suffrage Association. Member of the National Women's Hall of Fame. Spoke to national audiences urging passage of the Nineteenth Amendment. Adept at handling anti-suffrage arguments, she responded to criticism that equated male suffrage with military service by pointing out that "women bear armies." https://tennesseeencyclopedia.net/entries/anne-dallas-dudley

Crystal Catherine Eastman, 1881–1928

Co-founder of the Women's International League for Peace and Freedom in 1915 and co-founder of the American Civil Liberties Union in 1920. Best known for her leadership during the American suffragist movement. Inducted into the National Women's Hall of Fame in Seneca Falls, New York, in 2001. https://www.britannica.com/biography/Crystal-Eastman

Lizzie Crozier French, 1851–1926

Organizer of the Knoxville Equal Suffrage Association, president of the Tennessee Equal Suffrage Association and the Tennessee Federation of Women's Clubs, and state chair of the National Woman's Party. Opened and directed the East Tennessee Female Institute. https://tennesseeencyclopedia.net/entries/lizzie-crozier-french/

Betty Friedan, 1921–2006

A leading figure in the women's movement in the United States, her 1963 book *The Feminine Mystique* is often credited with sparking the second wave of American feminism in the twentieth century.

In 1966, Friedan co-founded and was elected the first president of the National Organization for Women (NOW), which aimed to bring women "into the mainstream of American society now [in] fully equal partnership with men." https://www.womenshistory.org/education-resources/biographies/betty-friedan

Abby Kelley Foster, 1811–1887
Abolitionist and leader of the feminist movement during the early to mid-nineteenth century. She spoke at the women's rights convention, held in 1848 in Seneca Falls, New York, and later played a key role at the first National Women's Rights Convention held in 1850 in Worcester, Massachusetts. https://www.womenofthehall.org/inductee/abby-kelley-foster/

Margaret Fuller, 1810–1850
Author of *Woman in the Nineteenth Century* (1845), which examined the place of women within society. Urged young women to seek greater independence from the home and family and to obtain such independence through education. https://www.britannica.com/biography/Margaret-Fuller

Charlotte Perkins Gilman, 1860–1935
Authored feminist utopian novel *Herland* (1915), where she introduced her readers to a country of women who worked cooperatively. Railed against the condition of women who were relegated to a life of confining costume and care for child and home. She envisioned a world in which women were free from the drudgery of cooking and cleaning and could engage in intellectual pursuits—a world in which women

threw off their corsets and breathed freely. https://www.radcliffe.
harvard.edu/schlesinger-library/exhibition/woman-human-life-
and-work-charlotte-perkins-gilman

Ruth Bader Ginsburg, 1933–2020

Supreme Court justice from 1993 until her death in 2020. First female professor at Columbia to earn tenure. Directed Women's Rights Project of the American Civil Liberties Union during the 1970s, when she led the fight against gender discrimination and successfully argued six landmark cases before the US Supreme Court. https://www.oyez.org/justices/ruth_bader_ginsburg

bell hooks (Gloria Jean Watkins), 1952–

American author, feminist, and social activist. Focus of her writing has been the intersectionality of race, capitalism, and gender, and what she describes as their ability to produce and perpetuate systems of oppression and class domination. In 2014, she founded the bell hooks Institute. http://www.bellhooksinstitute.com

Rear Admiral Grace Hopper, 1906–1992

Mother of computing. Her development of the first computer compiler and the first computer programming language helped revolutionize the world of computers. While trying to repair a Mark I computer, she discovered a moth caught in a relay. She taped the moth in the log book and from that coined the phrase "a bug in the computer." Owing to the breadth of her accomplishment as a pioneering computer scientist and to her naval rank, she is sometimes referred to as "Amazing Grace." A United States Navy destroyer is named in her honor. https://www.history.navy.mil/browse-by-topic/people/namesakes/grace-hopper.html

Barbara Jordan, 1936–1996

First Black state senator (from Texas) in the United States since 1883 as well as the first Black Southern woman ever elected to the US House of Representatives. In 1972, Jordan's peers elected her president *pro tempore* of the Texas senate, making her the first Black woman in America to preside over a legislative body. In 1976, she became the first woman and the first Black keynote speaker at a Democratic National Convention. https://history.house.gov/People/Detail/16031

Harriet Martineau, 1802–1876

The first female sociologist and British social theorist. She wrote *Society in America*, which included criticism of women's education: "The intellect of women is confined by an unjustifiable restriction of . . . education . . . As women have none of the objects in life for which an enlarged education is considered requisite, the education is not given . . . The choice is to either be ill-educated, passive, and subservient, or well-educated, vigorous, and free only upon sufferance." https://www.britannica.com/biography/Harriet-Martineau

Elizabeth Avery Meriwether, 1824–1916

Author, publisher, and prominent early activist in the woman suffrage movement, including important work in Memphis after the Civil War. Inspired to vote in 1873 by Susan B. Anthony. Presented suffrage petitions at both Democratic and Republican national conventions in 1880. http://historic-memphis.com/biographies/eliz-meriwether/eliz-meriwether.html

Lucretia Mott, 1793–1880

After being excluded from the World Anti-Slavery Convention in London in 1840, she turned her energy to increasing the station that women had in society. She participated in the first meeting about women's rights in Seneca Falls, New York, in 1848. She spoke out in favor of woman suffrage the rest of her life. Served as the first president of the American Equal Rights Association. https://www.womenshistory.org/education-resources/biographies/lucretia-mott

Maud Wood Park, 1871–1955

First president of the National League of Women Voters and leading congressional lobbyist for woman suffrage. https://suffragistmemorial.org/november-2015-suffragist-of-the-month

Alice Stokes Paul, 1885–1977

Helped secure the passage of the Nineteenth Amendment in 1920, guaranteeing women's right to vote. Led the National Woman's Party for more than fifty years and fought for the Equal Rights Amendment. Also helped ensure women were included as a protected class in the 1964 Civil Rights Act. https://socialwelfare.library.vcu.edu/people/paul-alice-stokes

J. Frankie Pierce, 1864–1954

Founder of the Tennessee Vocational School for Colored Girls. President of the Negro Women's Reconstruction League, the founder of the Nashville Federation of Colored Women's Clubs, and on the first Committee of Management of the Blue Triangle League of the YWCA. https://tennesseeencyclopedia.net/entries/juno-frankie-pierce

Jeannette Pickering Rankin, 1880–1973

First woman, and one of the few suffragists, elected to Congress. The only member of Congress to vote against US participation in both World War I and World War II. https://history.house.gov/People/Listing/R/RANKIN,-Jeannette-(R000055)/

Anna Howard Shaw, 1847–1919

Minister, physician, ardent feminist, and masterful orator. Campaigned for the League of Nations to promote world peace. https://www.womenofthehall.org/inductee/anna-howard-shaw

Elizabeth Cady Stanton, 1815–1902

Leader for woman suffrage and an abolitionist. She presented a Declaration of Sentiments in 1848 at the Seneca Falls Convention. She was the president of the National Woman Suffrage Association, 1892–1900. Along with a committee of twenty-six other women, she published *The Woman's Bible*, a two-volume commentary that challenged the notion that women should be subservient to men, as practiced by many religions. https://www.womenshistory.org/education-resources/biographies/elizabeth-cady-stanton

Gloria Steinem, 1934–

Writer, speaker, activist, and feminist organizer. Columnist for *New York* magazine and co-founder of *Ms.* magazine, where she remains a consulting editor. http://www.gloriasteinem.com/about

Lucy Stone, 1818–1893

In 1850, two years after the Seneca Falls Women's Rights Convention, Stone organized the first national Women's Rights Convention in Worcester, Massachusetts. Defied gender norms when she famously wrote marriage vows to reflect her egalitarian beliefs and refused to take her husband's last name. https://www.womenshistory.org/education-resources/biographies/lucy-stone

Mary Church Terrell, 1863–1954

Daughter of former slaves. Black activist who championed racial equality and woman suffrage. Her activism was sparked in 1892 when an old friend, Thomas Moss, was lynched in Memphis by whites because his business competed with theirs. Terrell joined Ida B. Wells-Barnett in anti-lynching campaigns. Helped found the National Association of Colored Women in 1896 and served as the organization's president from 1896 to 1901. In 1909, she was among the founders and charter members of the National Association for the Advancement of Colored People. https://www.womenshistory.org/education-resources/biographies/mary-church-terrell

Greta Thunberg, 2003–

Although not known for her feminist work, she displays feminist qualities as a brave young woman who stands up to world leaders, challenging their policies that harm the environment. Her work fighting climate change led to her inclusion in the *Time* 100 most influential people and the youngest person to ever be named *Time* Person of the Year. In 2019, *Forbes* listed her as one of the world's most powerful women.

Sojourner Truth, 1797–1883

Abolitionist and women's rights activist. Born into slavery but escaped with her infant daughter to freedom in 1826 and went to court to recover her son in 1828, becoming the first black woman to win such a case against a white man. At the Ohio Women's Rights Convention in 1851, she delivered a speech that became widely known during the Civil War by the title "Ain't I a Woman?" In 2014, Truth was included in *Smithsonian* magazine's list of the "100 Most Significant Americans of All Time."[45]

Alice Walker, 1944–

Author of *The Color Purple* in 1982, which earned a Pulitzer Prize and the National Book Club award. Her term "womanist" is used to describe a Black feminist.[46] "Womanism gives us a word of our own." She is the co-founder of a feminist publishing company, Wild Tree Press.

Ida Bell Wells-Barnett, 1862–1931

Prominent journalist and activist in the late nineteenth and early twentieth centuries. Wells-Barnett also used her skills as a journalist to shed light on the conditions of Blacks throughout the South. Founding member of the National Association of Colored Women's Club, which dealt with civil rights and woman suffrage. https://www.womenshistory.org/education-resources/biographies/ida-b-wells-barnett

---

45. The Smithsonian, November 17, 2014, "Meet the 100 Most Significant Americans of All Time," retrieved September 14, 2015.

46. Wilma Mankiller and others, "Womanism," The Reader's Companion to US Women's History, December 1, 1998, SIRS Issue Researcher, Indian Hills Library, Oakland, NJ, January 9, 2013, p. 1.

Rebecca West (Dame Cicely Isabel Fairfield), 1892–1983

British writer who, as a journalist, encouraged support for woman suffrage through the feminist weeklies *Freewoman* and the *Clarion*.

Sue Shelton White, 1887–1943

Suffragist, equal rights advocate, attorney, and writer. Helped write the 1923 Equal Rights Amendment. Tennessee chair of the National Woman's Party and edited the organization's newspaper, the *Suffragist*. White achieved notoriety for participating in a suffrage demonstration in which the NWP burned President Woodrow Wilson in effigy. She was arrested and served five days in the Old Work House, a condemned jail. After her release, White joined the "Prison Special," a chartered railroad car that traveled around the country bringing the issue of woman suffrage to the people. https://tennesseeencyclopedia.net/entries/sue-shelton-white

Frances Elizabeth Caroline Willard, 1839–1898

Prominent suffragist and social progressive who battled against gender inequality and fought to give a voice to the disenfranchised. Under her leadership, the Woman's Christian Temperance Union fought for broad social reforms, including equal pay for equal work, an eight-hour work day, world peace, the protection of women and children in the workplace, kindergartens, mothers' clubs (the predecessor of the PTA), jail reform, uniform marriage and divorce laws, physical education in schools, higher education for women, choice of vocation, and equal opportunity. https://suffragistmemorial.org/frances-elizabeth-caroline-willard-1839-1898

Oprah Winfrey, 1954–
American media executive, actress, talk show host, television producer, and philanthropist. Best known for *The Oprah Winfrey Show*, which was the highest-rated television program of its kind in history and was nationally syndicated from 1986 to 2011 in Chicago. Considered by many to be one of the most influential women in the world. http://www.oprah.com

Photo: Lawrence Jackson/White House

Adeline Virginia Woolf (Stephen), 1882–1941
British author whose essay "A Room of One's Own" explores the struggle women have had striving for empowerment throughout history.

Mary Wollstonecraft, 1759–1797
English writer, philosopher, and advocate of women's rights. Best known for her 1792 work *A Vindication of the Rights of Woman*, in which she argues that women are not naturally inferior to men, but appear to be only because they lack education. She imagined a social order founded on reason. http://www.bbc.co.uk/history/british/empire_seapower/wollstonecraft_01.shtml

Malala Yousafzai, 1997–
Pakistani activist for female education and the youngest Nobel Prize laureate. Her advocacy has grown into an international movement, and according to former Pakistani Prime Minister Shahid Khaqan Abbasi, she has become "the most prominent citizen" of the country. https://www.malala.org

SUFFRAGETTE SERIES Nº II.

EVERYBODY
WORKS BUT
MOTHER
SHE'S A
SUFFRAGETT

I WANT TO VOTE, BUT
MY·WIFE·WONT·LET·ME
COPYRIGHTED, 1909. BY DUNSTON-WEILER LITHOGRAPH CO.

This 1909 card was number eleven in a twelve-card series of full-color lithographic postcards opposing woman suffrage.

Suffrage supporters stand with their horse-drawn wagon and sign proclaiming that "National American Woman Suffrage Association founded in 1869 supports Bristow-Mondell Resolution drafted by Susan B. Anthony, 1874, First, Last and Always."

4

Votes for Women!

"The right is ours. Have it we must. Use it we will."
—Elizabeth Cady Stanton, Seneca Falls, NY, 1848

A large part of the feminist history in the United States was the suffragist movement. It is hard to argue for equal rights if one doesn't have the right to vote. At the time of this writing, women had their franchise for barely 100 years in this country. It's no wonder that equality is still elusive.

Perhaps Elaine Weiss wrote it best in her book *The Woman's Hour: The Great Fight to Win the Vote*. "Winning the vote required seventy-two years of ceaseless agitation by three generations of dedicated, fearless suffragists, who sought to overturn centuries of law and millennia of tradition concerning gender roles. The women who launched the movement were dead by the time it was completed; the women who secured its final success weren't born when it began."[47]

---

47. Elaine Weiss, *The Woman's Hour: The Great Fight to Win the Vote*, New York City: Penguin Random House, 2018.

This quote is similar to how Carrie Chapman Catt described the seven-decade struggle for suffrage: "Young suffragists who helped forge the last links of that chain were not born when it began. Old suffragists who forged the first links were dead when it ended."[48]

The Nineteenth Amendment to the US Constitution was ratified on August 18, 1920, when Tennessee provided the thirty-sixth state approval required for passage. "It also marked the climax of 72 years of ceaseless campaigning by four generations of American women activists," according to *The Perfect 36: Tennessee Delivers Woman Suffrage*.[49]

The Nineteenth Amendment reads, "The right of citizens of the United States to vote shall not be denied or abridged by the United States or by any State on account of sex." This wording is nearly identical to the language used in the Fifteenth Amendment, ratified in 1870, which guaranteed the right of Black men to vote. Although fifty years separated the passage of the Fifteenth and Nineteenth Amendments, the struggles for suffrage for both women and Black men were intertwined for much longer.

Many leaders of the women's rights movement were also deeply involved in abolitionism in the early to mid-nineteenth century and were in favor of guaranteeing voting rights for Black men following the Civil War. However, the support from women's rights advocates was not universal, due to competing priorities between organizations as well as persistent racism that continued throughout society at that time.

"Power concedes nothing without a demand," insisted the great universal suffragist Frederick Douglass, and he taught this essential lesson to the early advocates of votes for women.[50]

---

48. Weiss, *The Woman's Hour*.

49. Carol Lynn Yellin and Janann Sherman, *The Perfect 36: Tennessee Delivers Woman Suffrage*, Oak Ridge, TN: Iris Press, 1998.

50. Weiss, *The Woman's Hour*.

Beginning in the 1840s, many women's rights groups demanded suffrage as part of their desire for equality. At the Seneca Falls Convention of 1848, a woman suffrage resolution was passed, even though some members voted against the measure, believing it was too extreme. A drive for women's voting rights continued with the first National Women's Rights Convention in 1850.

During the Civil War, much of the attention for suffrage waned, but in 1869, the first national suffrage organizations were formed. Susan B. Anthony and Elizabeth Cady Stanton established the National Woman Suffrage Association. Lucy Stone, Julia Ward Howe, Henry Blackwell, and others formed the American Woman Suffrage Association.

The major disagreement between the two organizations was whether the Fifteenth Amendment should include voting rights for women as well as Black men.

The partisan rivalries between these two organizations persisted until the two groups set aside their differences to form the National American Woman Suffrage Association in 1890. While this and other organizations pushed for a change in the laws at the national and state levels, many of the same suffragists chose an additional path by attempting to vote and filing lawsuits when they were denied their rights to do so.

In 1872, Anthony was arrested after voting. Even though she was found guilty, her trial's publicity provided a spark to the suffrage movement.

In 1875, the Supreme Court ruled against a woman's right to vote, which renewed a focus to pass an amendment to the US Constitution as well as to change laws in individual states.

To gain a better appreciation for the long struggle for woman suffrage in America, it's helpful to look back at some of the earliest known votes by women.

According to an address delivered by Judge Henry Chapin in 1864, a wealthy widow, Lydia Taft, voted in town meetings in

Uxbridge, Massachusetts, in 1756. After the nation's independence, there are records of other women landowners who were allowed to vote; however, the first state to enfranchise women was New Jersey, which allowed all adults who owned a specific amount of property to vote. Later in the 1790s, laws in New Jersey referred to voters as "he" or "she," and records show that women regularly voted. Just a few years later, in 1807, the state rescinded women's franchise.[51]

Thirty years after New Jersey passed a law that excluded women from voting, Kentucky passed a law allowing a woman to vote if certain conditions were met (e.g., head of household, over twenty-one years of age, paid property taxes).

To truly appreciate the struggle for woman suffrage, one must go back even further to learn how women first had to gain the right to speak in a public setting. Anthony is quoted as saying, "No advanced step taken by women has been so bitterly contested as that of speaking in public. For nothing which they have attempted, not even to secure the suffrage, have they been so abused, condemned and antagonized."[52]

As part of the abolition movement, women were often prohibited from speaking out at public meetings or even in private meetings where men and women were both in attendance. Some of this was due to an interpretation of Christian scriptures that did not allow for women to teach men and instructed women to remain silent in church. Perhaps to help counter this injustice, Stanton later published *The Woman's Bible* in 1895, where she argued against using the Bible to subjugate women as inferior to men.

Nearly a century later, I would be taught similar "women are the weaker sex" doctrine while attending a Christian church

---

51. Judith Wellman, *The Road to Seneca Falls: Elizabeth Cady Stanton and the First Woman's Rights Convention*, Champaign, IL: University of Illinois Press, 2010.

52. S. McMillen, *Seneca Falls and the Origins of the Women's Rights Movement*, New York City: Oxford University Press, 2009.

in the 1980s and 1990s. There are no doubt places in America where women's silence and deference to men as the head of their household are still commanded from pulpits today.

Often, basic human rights were denied to women based on an interpretation of common law. For example, legal scholar William Blackstone wrote, "By marriage, the husband and wife are one person in law: that is, the very being or legal existence of the woman is suspended during the marriage."[53]

North Carolina's Supreme Court denied a woman's request for divorce in 1862 because "the law gives the husband power to use such a degree of force necessary to make the wife behave and know her place."[54] This ruling was especially appalling because the woman was seeking a divorce after her husband had horsewhipped her.

Lucy Stone had her household goods forcibly sold at auction by the local constable when she refused to pay taxes in 1857. Stone argued that it was unfair for women to be taxed without enjoying the right to vote on laws that affected the taxes.[55]

As a practical matter for woman suffrage organizers, laws restricted a woman's ability to legally sign a contract. Can you imagine trying to rent a place to meet or print programs without the ability to enter into a contract?

Some contract and property laws were changed not because of a concern for women's rights, but because men were not keen on turning over control of their wealth—such as a daughter's inheritance—to some future son-in-law.

It should be noted that not all supporters of women's rights supported their right to vote. During the 1848 Seneca Falls Convention, all resolutions were unanimously approved by the 300

53. McMillen, *Seneca Falls*.

54. Ida Husted Harper, *Life and Work of Susan B. Anthony*, New York City: Creative Media Partners, 1898.

55. McMillen, *Seneca Falls*.

male and female attendees except for the resolution calling for a woman's right to vote. It was introduced by Stanton but was adopted only after abolitionist leader Frederick Douglass voiced his support.[56]

Even Anthony, who is arguably the most noted suffragist in American history, was not always in favor of making enfranchisement the first priority in the overall struggle for equal rights. "I wasn't ready to vote, didn't want to vote, but I did want equal pay for equal work."[57]

Prior to the Civil War, Anthony and others prioritized their abolitionist work above their desire for their own suffrage. During the Civil War, Anthony led the first national women's political organization, called the Women's Loyal National League, which collected nearly 400,000 signatures supporting abolition. This was the largest petition drive in the US up to that time.[58]

After the Civil War, a new approach to suffrage emerged after the Fourteenth Amendment passed in 1868. The strategy, known as the New Departure, was based on an argument that women were already entitled to vote thanks to a passage in the Fourteenth Amendment that reads, "All persons born or naturalized in the United States, and subject to the jurisdiction thereof, are citizens of the United States and of the State wherein they reside. No State shall make or enforce any law which shall abridge the privileges or immunities of citizens of the United States; nor shall any State deprive any person of life, liberty, or property, without due process of law; nor deny to any person within its jurisdiction the equal protection of the laws."[59]

---

56. McMillen, *Seneca Falls*.

57. National Woman Suffrage Association, Report of the International Council of Women, Volume 1, 1888, p. 327.

58. Wendy Hamand Venet, *Neither Ballots nor Bullets: Women Abolitionists and the Civil War*, Charlottesville, VA: University Press of Virginia, 1991.

59. E. C. DuBois, *Feminism and Suffrage: The Emergence of an Independent Women's Movement in America, 1848-1869*, Ithaca, NY: Cornell University Press, 1978.

In other words, they argued, no further action was required for women to vote because the Constitution, as changed by the Fourteenth Amendment, already provided for woman suffrage.

This position, first argued in 1869 by Missouri couple Francis and Virginia Minor, was adopted in 1871 by the National Woman Suffrage Association. Women were encouraged to attempt to vote but were mostly turned away or had their votes invalidated. The US District Court in Washington, DC, ruled that women did not have the right to vote, writing, "The fact that the practical working of the assumed right would be destructive of civilization is decisive that the right does not exist."[60]

The New Departure strategy ended in 1875 when the Supreme Court ruled in *Minor v. Happersett* that "the Constitution of the United States does not confer the right of suffrage upon anyone."[61]

The NWSA decided to pursue the far more difficult strategy of campaigning for a constitutional amendment that would guarantee voting rights for women.[62]

A famous example of the New Departure strategy was Anthony's attempt to vote in the presidential election of 1872. She was arrested and found guilty. Although she was not allowed to speak during her trial, she did respond after being found guilty, by saying, ". . . you have trampled underfoot every vital principle of our government. My natural rights, my civil rights, my political rights, my judicial rights, are all alike ignored."[63]

When the judge ordered her to pay a $100 fine, Anthony

60. A. D. Gordon, "The Trial of Susan B. Anthony: A Short Narrative," Federal Judicial Center, retrieved June 4, 2019.

61. Elizabeth Cady Stanton, Susan B. Anthony, and Matilda Joslyn Gage, *History of Woman Suffrage*, Rochester, NY: Charles Mann, 1887.

62. Kermit L. Hall and others, *The Oxford Companion to the Supreme Court of the United States*, New York City: Oxford University Press, 2005.

63. Harper, *Life and Work of Susan B. Anthony*.

responded, "I shall never pay a dollar of your unjust penalty." She was true to her promise and the matter was dropped without further penalty.[64]

Six years after Anthony's act of civil disobedience, her friend, Senator Aaron A. Sargent, introduced a constitutional amendment into Congress. Forty years later, the Nineteenth Amendment to the Constitution would finally pass. The wording for the amendment would not change and was essentially the same as the wording for the Fifteenth Amendment, except the word "sex" replaced the words "race, color, or previous condition of servitude."

Although women could not vote nationally until 1920, there were places in America, especially in the West, where women's enfranchisement was secured, including the Wyoming Territory in 1869, Utah in 1870, Colorado in 1893, and Idaho in 1896.[65]

The struggle for woman suffrage was tedious and hard-fought, requiring an inordinate amount of patience and perseverance. For example, there were 480 campaigns in 33 states between 1870 and 1910, resulting in only 17 ballot initiatives. This forty-year effort resulted in suffrage for exactly two states, Colorado and Idaho.

Opposition to woman suffrage came from many fronts. Brewers and distillers were concerned that women voters would put them out of business through the prohibition of alcohol.

In addition to businesses that profited off the sale of alcohol, other businesses that profited off child labor opposed giving women the right to vote. An example was Southern cotton mills, in addition to others interested in preserving their profits. "Suffrage rhetoric claimed that enfranchised women would outlaw child labor, pass minimum-wage and maximum-hours laws for women workers,

---

64. Harper, *Life and Work of Susan B. Anthony.*

65. Dawn Langan Teele, "How the West Was Won: Competition, Mobilization, and Women's Enfranchisement in the United States," *The Journal of Politics* 80, no. 2 (April 2018): 442-461.

and establish health and safety standards for factory workers." The threat of these reforms united planters, textile mill owners, railroad magnates, city machine bosses, and the liquor interest in a formidable combine against suffrage.[66]

Some religious organizations opposed women's voting rights because they feared a breakdown in traditional family roles.

Bishop O'Connell of Boston, in an address on the mission for men, said, ". . . There is no doubt that one of the main causes of this sinister feminism of which we read so much and see quoted enough, is what would appear to be a growing weakness on the part of the manhood of the nation. The very fact that women are so often clamoring to take all power and authority into their hands is certainly no compliment to the manhood of the nation. . . . After all, women, the wife, and the children, expect a father to have and to exercise the rightful authority due to his position. But if he abdicates that position . . . well, no one can be surprised if, little by little, women learn to do without the authority of man and to usurp a great deal of it themselves. That leads to a false feminism which certainly, unless it is curbed in time, will have disastrous results for humanity, because it is unnatural. . . ."[67]

Many political party leaders did not want to give up the power they had over male voters, so they also opposed woman suffrage.

One political cartoon summed it up this way: "The more a politician allows himself to be henpecked, the more henpecking we will have in politics. A vote for federal suffrage is a vote for organized female nagging forever."[68]

---

66. Elna C. Green, *Southern Strategies: Southern Women and the Woman Suffrage Questions,* Chapel Hill, NC: University of North Carolina Press, 1997.

67. Reprinted in the *New York World*, March 9, 1920, and circulated by suffrage opponents during the ratification struggle in Nashville in August 1920, as cited in Yellin and Sherman, 1998, p. 43.

68. Yellin and Sherman, *The Perfect 36*, p. 65.

Even the *New York Times* reversed its support for women's rights through an editorial published in 1912 that warned that if women earned the right to vote they would also want to serve as "soldiers and sailors, police patrolmen or firemen … and would serve on juries and elect themselves to executive offices and judgeships." The editorial also encouraged men to fight back or suffer the consequences of women voting, "if the men are not firm and wise enough and, it may as well be said, masculine enough to prevent them."[69]

The opposition even extended to women who opposed allowing their fellow female citizens to vote. The Woman's Anti-Suffrage Association of Washington formally organized in 1870, spread to twenty states, and reorganized as the National Association Opposed to Woman Suffrage in 1911. The group, known as 'antis,' spoke out against woman suffrage, feminism, and socialism, arguing that women voting "would reduce the special protections and routes of influence available to women, destroy the family, and increase the number of socialist-leaning voters."[70]

It was as divisive as many of the issues we find contentious today.

"There were powerful forces opposing federal woman suffrage as it approached the legal finish line: political, corporate, and ideological adversaries intent upon stopping the Nineteenth Amendment. Like the key sociopolitical issues of today—from reproductive rights to same-sex marriage—attitudes toward woman suffrage divided communities, families, and friends, thrusting women into opposing camps," author Elaine Weiss wrote.[71]

Those forces who opposed woman suffrage go all the way back to the leaders most of us know as founding fathers. " 'We the People' really meant, 'We the White, Wealthy Men.' Despite much

---

69. Sarah Grimké, "The Equality of the Sexes and the Condition of Women," 1838, as cited in Flexner (1959), pp. 43, 348 n.19.

70. Grimké, "The Equality of the Sexes."

71. Weiss, *The Woman's Hour.*

lofty rhetoric, all men were not created equal, and women didn't count at all," according to Weiss.[72]

In spite of the opposition from many well-funded and well-organized groups, the tide in favor of woman suffrage began to shift in the second decade of the twentieth century. Theodore Roosevelt's Progressive Party endorsed the right of women to vote in 1912, and the growing socialist movement also endorsed woman suffrage.

The National American Woman Suffrage Association claimed two million members in 1916, the same year that both the Republican and Democratic parties endorsed the vote for women. The endorsement, however, was supported state by state, rather than nationally. This was consistent with the strategy evoked by NAWSA and others, partly to assuage the fears of Southerners. The leader of NAWSA, Carrie Chapman Catt, shifted strategies, calling for a plan for national suffrage. A year later, Miriam Leslie donated nearly one million dollars to support the cause, which Catt used to form the Leslie Woman Suffrage Commission.[73]

Suffrage was part of a larger call for women's independence in the late nineteenth century—a call answered by a younger group of women who were not content to play the same subservient, self-oppressive role their mothers played. Something as simple as riding a bicycle increased a woman's mobility, while simultaneously rejecting traditional notions of a woman's weakness.

Susan B. Anthony said bicycles had "done more to emancipate women than anything else in the world."[74]

---

72. Weiss, *The Woman's Hour.*

73. Timeline and Map of Woman Suffrage Legislation State by State, 1838-1919, University of Washington, retrieved June 5, 2019, http://depts.washington.edu/moves/WomanSuffrage_map.shtml

74. Marjorie S. Wheeler, *New Women of the New South: The Leaders of the Woman Suffrage Movement in the Southern States,* New York City: Oxford Press, 1993.

This was the cover of a program promoting the National American Woman Suffrage Association march to the US Capitol in 1913.

Elizabeth Cady Stanton said, "Woman is riding to suffrage on the bicycle."[75]

These new roles for women, which many saw as unladylike, manifested into campaigns for voting rights, such as marching in parades, speaking from soap boxes on street corners, and hiking long distances to gain attention for their cause.

In 1912, suffrage supporters marched 170 miles over 12 days to New York's capitol to deliver petitions to the governor. A year later, the "Army of the Hudson" marched 250 miles over 16 days from New York to Washington.

The change in women's roles accelerated during World War I, when men deployed overseas and had to be replaced in the

---

75. Wheeler, *New Women*.

Library of Congress
Suffragists demonstrate against Woodrow Wilson in Chicago in 1916.

workforce, even in places where women traditionally had not served, such as steel mills and production plants. NAWSA supported the war effort; however, women's support was not unanimous. Notably, the first woman in Congress, Montana's Representative Jeannette Rankin, voted against the declaration of war in 1916.

After the "war to end all wars" concluded, some believed that it was a national disgrace that a beacon of democracy and freedom like the United States did not permit half its citizens to enjoy the right to vote. After all, women in more than twenty other nations, including Germany, had already earned the right to vote.

President Woodrow Wilson supported suffrage before the Senate in 1918, saying, "We have made partners of the women in this war; shall we admit them only to a partnership of suffering and sacrifice and toil and not to a partnership of privilege and right?"[76]

---

76. Woodrow Wilson, *The Public Papers of Woodrow Wilson: War and Peace; Presidential Messages, Addresses, and Public Paper* (1917-1924), p. 265, quoted in Flexner (1959), p. 302.

Wilson's support was not guaranteed, and neither was support in Congress. In 1915, the House defeated a suffrage bill, 201 to 174. Three years later, a suffrage bill garnered the two-thirds majority needed, with only one vote to spare, but the bill failed to earn the required two-thirds majority in the Senate, falling two votes short. The Senate took up the bill again in 1919, but it failed the two-thirds majority requirement by one vote.

Many politicians wanted the amendment passed in time for women to vote in the 1920 election, so President Wilson called a special session of Congress. The bill passed comfortably in the House on May 21, 1919, with 42 votes to spare (304 in favor and 89 against). The Senate followed on June 4, 1919, with 56 in favor and 25 against.

The fight for suffrage was far from over. In fact, the broader national fight had just begun, because passage of the Nineteenth Amendment required approval in thirty-six states.

By March 1920, thirty-five of the necessary thirty-six states had ratified the amendment. However, the road to woman suffrage would eventually run through the South.

This posed several problems. For example, most Southern white men held conservative values opposed to a public role for women. There was also the fierce defense of states' rights, meaning that any perceived influence from a national level would suffer innate opposition. Finally, an extension of voting rights to women naturally meant that Black women would be voting, and any dilution of the white vote was unacceptable in a society still reeling from the Civil War and Reconstruction.

An example of the Southern suffrage opposition is a 1914 speech before the Georgia state legislature by Mildred Rutherford, president of the Georgia United Daughters of the Confederacy. "The women who are working for this measure are striking at the principle for which their fathers fought during the Civil War," Rutherford said. "Woman's suffrage comes from the North and the West and from women who do not believe in states' rights and who wish to see negro women using the ballot. I do not believe the state of Georgia has sunk so low that her good men cannot legislate for women. If this time ever comes, then it will be time for women to claim the ballot."[77]

Eventually, enough states would vote in favor of the Nineteenth Amendment, with the state of Tennessee serving as the crucial thirty-sixth vote needed for passage. When she arrived to garner support for passage, Carrie Chapman Catt told reporters, "All the states consider Tennessee the queen of the Southern states and the leader in all progressive matters.

"Suffrage supporters feel certain that Tennessee will rise to the occasion and use its decisive vote for the women. The eyes of the country and the world are centered here at Nashville."[78]

Another prominent figure who fought for passage in Tennessee was Anne Dallas Dudley. She came from a very prominent family, as the naming of a certain Texas city confirms.

Dudley was the first woman in Tennessee to make an open-air speech, which she did after leading a suffrage parade in May 1914. While arguing against the notion that "because only men bear arms, only men should vote," Dudley refuted, "Yes, but women bear armies."[79]

Working separately for the same goal was a woman from a completely different background.

Orphaned at fourteen, Sue Shelton White attended the West Tennessee Business College and was to become Tennessee's first female court reporter. According to a 1920 report in the *Chattanooga*

77. Marjorie S. Wheeler, *New Women of the New South: The Leaders of the Woman Suffrage Movement in the Southern States*, New York City: Oxford Press, 1993.

78. Weiss, *The Woman's Hour.*

79. Tennessee Woman Suffrage Monument, retrieved May 18, 2019, http://tnsuffragemonument.org/

News, "Her fragile strength is evident. Her frail fingers will never lift anything heavier than a ballot to obtain her rights."[80]

When commenting about Tennessee, White told Alice Paul, "The more I look into the Tennessee situation, the more I realize that we face a terrific fight. The anti-suffragists have already begun work, appealing, as they always do in Southern campaigns, to deeply seated prejudices and pouring vitriol into old wounds." Unless suffragists committed themselves fully and fought relentlessly, Tennessee was in danger of being lost. And perhaps, with it, the amendment.[81]

On September 14, 1920, Connecticut passed the amendment. Other states followed years later: Vermont, 1921; Delaware, 1923; Maryland, 1941; Virginia, 1952; Alabama, 1953; Florida and South Carolina, 1969; Georgia and Louisiana, 1970; and North Carolina, 1971. Finally, sixty-four years after the law originally passed, Mississippi ratified the Nineteenth Amendment in 1984.

Let's return to Tennessee for a moment to relive some of the drama surrounding the crucial fight for ratification in Nashville.

Woman visionary Paula Casey introduced me to *The Perfect 36: Tennessee Delivers Woman Suffrage,* written by Carol Lynn Yellin and Janann Sherman. Casey is a dynamo whose contributions to the memory of woman suffrage specifically and to equal rights for all more generally offer a living legacy which I greatly admire.

A quote I discovered during my research for this book was from Casey, who said, "What these women did was magnificent. These women were the greatest politicians the world has ever seen because they won the right to vote without even having the right to vote."[82]

---

80. B. Carey, *The Tennessee Magazine,* 2019.

81. Weiss, *The Woman's Hour.*

82. John Beifuss, "A Downtown Monument Celebrating Memphis Women," *USA Today Network,* March 2, 2018, retrieved June 18, 2018, https://www.commercialappeal.com/story/news/2018/03/02/beifuss-file-downtown-monument-celebrating-memphis-women/374529002/

I like the quote because it embodies the audacious tenacity women suffragists showed in their struggle to earn a right to vote, a struggle that came to a heated climax in the Tennessee capital during the sweltering summer of 1920.

According to Yellin and Sherman, there was a showdown in Nashville in the months leading up to the historic suffrage vote, a showdown that climaxed with a floor vote in the Tennessee House that could have gone either way.

The showdown was predicated by thirty-five other states ratifying the Nineteenth Amendment, leaving just one more for passage. Six states, all from the South, had already rejected ratification. Only seven states had not yet voted on the matter. Three of these states—Florida, Louisiana, and North Carolina— seemed unlikely to approve of something that many believed violated state sovereignty. Wounds were still fresh from the Civil War, also known locally as the War of Northern Aggression.

Tennessee, a North-South border state, had just adjourned its legislative session after granting partial suffrage to women (presidential and municipal elections). Would it be possible to call a special session to expand the suffrage to full voting rights? It depended a great deal on the governor, Albert Roberts, who happened to be running for re-election. He agreed to call a special session only after the August 5 primary, though "in ample time for women to vote in the 1920 elections."[83]

Heavy hitters from both sides of the argument descended on the Tennessee capital in the summer of 1920, including Carrie Chapman Catt, who arrived on July 17, expecting to stay a few days, as evidenced by the one small bag she carried off the train. Instead she stayed for six weeks to see passage through to victory.

As legislators arrived in Nashville, they were met by suffrage proponents offering yellow roses and by anti-suffragists who offered

83. Yellin and Sherman, *The Perfect 36.*

red roses. This is why some refer to the Tennessee ratification fight as the War of the Roses.

Those opposed to suffrage claimed that ratification of the Nineteenth Amendment was "the first step toward socialism, free love, and the breakup of the American family."[84]

As I read this dire warning 100 years after it was projected, I found it interesting how many times these hyperbolic false predictions have been used to foil progress in the past and how many times they would continue to be used to keep those without power in their place.

Other language used to oppose the women's vote included propaganda claiming that all suffragists were "atheistic feminists who rewrote the Bible, destroyed the home, and blackened the honor of Robert E. Lee."[85]

It's amazing how those without a rational, valid argument stoop to ad hominem attacks and fear-based claims. If one looks around today, these same tactics may look very familiar.

The specific details of the back-and-forth in the Tennessee legislature between August 9 and August 18 can be found elsewhere; however, I would be remiss if I didn't note that passage essentially came down to the vote of one young man who listened to the pleadings of his mother, who wrote, "Dear Son: Hurrah, and vote for suffrage!"[86]

This young man was twenty-four-year-old Harry Burn, who said, "I know that a mother's advice is always safest for her boy to follow, and my mother wanted me to vote for ratification."[87]

After the Nineteenth Amendment passed, interest in women's rights waned.

---

84. Yellin and Sherman, *The Perfect 36.*

85. Yellin and Sherman, *The Perfect 36.*

86. Yellin and Sherman, *The Perfect 36.*

87. Yellin and Sherman, *The Perfect 36.*

The National American Woman Suffrage Association became the League of Women Voters and the National Woman's Party began work on the Equal Rights Amendment, which passed Congress in 1972 but was never ratified by the required number of states.

So, what effect did woman suffrage have on politics and policy? In the beginning, politicians did address issues of interest to women, such as children's health and public schools. However, when it came time to vote, women generally shared the same views and voted similarly as men.[88]

Women also voted in fewer numbers than their male counterparts until 1980; since then women have often voted in higher percentages.

The effect had lasting impact beyond voting rights for women.

"The crusade for woman suffrage stands as one of the defining civil rights movements in the history of our country, and its organizing strategies, lobbying techniques, and nonviolent protest actions became the model for the civil rights campaigns to follow in the twentieth and twenty-first centuries," according to Weiss's *The Woman's Hour.*[89]

---

88. Kristi Andersen, *After Suffrage: Women in Partisan and Electoral Politics before the New Deal*, University of Chicago Press, 1996.

89. Weiss, *The Woman's Hour.*

Activist Phyllis Schlafly, wearing a 'Stop ERA' badge, demonstrates with other women against the Equal Rights Amendment in front of the White House in 1977 in Washington, DC. Schlafly and her supporters used housewife symbolism promoting traditional roles to fight the amendment.

5

Equal Rights Amendment

"**E**quality of rights under the law shall not be denied or abridged by the United States or by any state on account of sex."

This is the text of the Equal Rights Amendment, which seems pretty simple and without controversy to me, and I suspect to most other Americans. So why did the amendment, first proposed in 1923 and passed out of Congress in 1972, fail to earn ratification?

As with most issues, it's complicated.

Many religious conservatives argued that the ERA would lead to homosexual marriage and universal abortion rights. Other opponents resisted a change to traditional gender roles, which they believed could lead to women fighting in combat and could even change laws that required only men to register for selective service (formerly the draft).

One opponent in particular was most effective playing to conservative traditional values using housewife symbolism. Phyllis Schlafly and her supporters took homemade bread, jams, and apple pies to state legislators, sharing slogans such as "Preserve us from a congressional jam; Vote against the ERA sham" and "I am for Mom and apple pie."[90]

Opponents also appealed to married women, alleging that if the ERA were passed, it would mean the end to alimony and the tendency to grant mothers custody of children following a divorce.

Others argued that there was no need for the ERA because women were already equal to men following the passage of the Equal Pay Act of 1963 and the Civil Rights Act of 1964.[91]

The Alice Paul Institute offers a helpful summary on its website, www.equalrightsamendment.org:[92]

"The Equal Rights Amendment is a proposed amendment to the United States Constitution designed to guarantee equal legal rights for all American citizens regardless of sex. It seeks to end the legal distinctions between men and women in terms of divorce, property, employment, and other matters.

"While women enjoy more rights today than they did when the ERA was first introduced in 1923 or when it passed out of Congress in 1972, hard-won laws against sex discrimination do not rest on any unequivocal constitutional foundation. They can be inconsistently enforced or even repealed by a simple majority vote. Elements of sex discrimination remain in statutory and case law, and courts have had difficulty applying a consistent standard to gender-based classifications, which are not inherently suspect or comparable to racial or ethnic classifications under equal-protection analysis.

---

90. Donald T. Critchlow, *Phyllis Schlafly and Grassroots Conservatism: A Woman's Crusade*, Princeton, NJ: Princeton University Press, 2005.

91. Jane Perlez, "Plan to Omit Rights Amendment from Platform Brings Objections," *New York Times*, May 17, 1984, retrieved February 1, 2019.

92. The Alice Paul Institute and Equal Rights Amendment, retrieved February 5, 2019, www.equalrightsamendment.org.

"The need for a federal Equal Rights Amendment remains as compelling as it was in 1978, when now Supreme Court Justice Ruth Bader Ginsburg wrote in the *Harvard Women's Law Journal*: 'With the Equal Rights Amendment, we may expect Congress and the state legislatures to undertake in earnest, systematically and pervasively, the law revision so long deferred. And in the event of legislative default, the courts will have an unassailable basis for applying the bedrock principle: All men and all women are created equal.'"[93]

The Equal Rights Amendment was passed by Congress on March 22, 1972, and sent to the states for ratification. In order to be added to the Constitution, it needed approval by legislatures in three-fourths (thirty-eight) of the fifty states.

By 1977, the legislatures of thirty-five states had approved the amendment. In 1978, Congress voted to extend the original March 1979 deadline to June 30, 1982. However, no additional states voted yes before that date, and the ERA fell three states short of ratification.

The fifteen states that did not ratify the Equal Rights Amendment before the 1982 deadline were Alabama, Arizona, Arkansas, Florida, Georgia, Illinois, Louisiana, Mississippi, Missouri, Nevada, North Carolina, Oklahoma, South Carolina, Utah, and Virginia.

In 1994, activists formulated the "three-state strategy" for ratification. Under this plan, proponents say the ERA is still viable and needs only three new state ratifications to add to the thirty-five ratifications achieved before 1982. Since that strategy was formed, ERA bills have been introduced in subsequent years in one or more legislative sessions in ten of the unratified states (Arizona, Arkansas, Florida, Louisiana, Mississippi, Missouri, North Carolina, Oklahoma, Utah, and Virginia).

Between 1995 and 2016, ERA ratification bills were released

---

93. Alice Paul Institute, www.equalrightsamendment.org.

from committee in some states and were passed by one but not both houses of the legislature in two of them. In Illinois, the House but not the Senate passed an ERA ratification bill in 2003, while the Senate but not the House did so in 2014. In five of the six years between 2011 and 2016, the Virginia Senate passed a resolution ratifying the Equal Rights Amendment, but the House of Delegates never released a companion bill from committee for a full vote on the House floor.

On March 22, 2017, forty-five years to the day after Congress passed the ERA, Nevada became the thirty-sixth state to ratify it. On May 30, 2018, Illinois became the thirty-seventh state. On January 15, 2020, Virginia became the thirty-eighth state.

ERA bills have also been introduced in the legislatures of Arizona, Florida, North Carolina, Utah, and Virginia.

In January 2019, Representative Carolyn B. Maloney introduced a resolution that would propose a new Equal Rights Amendment. As of the writing of this book, it has not received the two-thirds support required in the House or the Senate. Even if it does receive that support, it would require thirty-eight states to ratify the amendment before it would become law.

"The #MeToo movement really has given the women's movement a lot of strength, but we now need to harness it into positive change," including finally passing the Equal Rights Amendment, Maloney said.[94]

Another tack, led by Representative Jackie Speier of California, would eliminate the ERA's ratification deadline.

When the 117th US Congress convened in January 2021, resolutions with bipartisan support were introduced to remove the time limit placed upon the ERA in 1972. On Wednesday, March 17, 2021, the House of Representatives voted to remove

---

94. Lara Weiss, "A New Era for the ERA?" *Roll Call*, May 23, 2019, retrieved June 3, 2019.

the time limit with a vote of 222 to 204 on House Joint Resolution 17. Attention now turns to the Senate and moving Senate Joint Resolution 1 to the floor for a vote.[95]

Have you ever wondered whether your state has ratified the Equal Rights Amendment? Wonder no more, because it's simple to find out by visiting https://www.equalrightsamendment.org/era-ratification-map. For states that have not ratified, the site also provides contact information for your senators.

On a personal note, I was born in New Mexico, raised in Texas, and live in Tennessee. I'm proud to say all three of those states ratified the ERA, although sadly Tennessee later voted to rescind its ratification, a measure that is legally questionable.

In America, we must lead by example in protecting women's rights and supporting their empowerment.
—Barack Obama, presidential proclamation, February 28, 2011

---

95. Weiss, "A New Era."

The Women's March was a worldwide protest on January 21, 2017, the day after Donald Trump's presidential inauguration. Prompted by Trump statements that many saw as offensive to women, it became one of the largest single-day protests in US history. The march focused on advocating women's rights, reproductive rights, immigration reform, healthcare reform, and other issues.

6

Reproductive Rights

In 1984 I was sitting in my high school library researching for a debate about abortion. Honestly, I hadn't really thought about the issue much as a teenager, but I was pretty certain that I was supposed to be against it. This was an advantage as a debater, because we're required to prepare both sides of the argument, affirmative and negative.

One quote I found made a lot of sense to me at the time, and I believe it applies to a lot of controversial issues. To paraphrase the quote as best I remember, "regardless of how much information is presented, the chances of changing someone's mind on this topic are near zero."

In the interest of self-disclosure, I will confess that my views on abortion have changed over the course of my lifetime. While at college, I joined a church and began learning that abortion was considered murder, because "thou didst form my inward parts, thou didst knit me together in my mother's womb" (Psalm 139:13). And, "Before I formed you in the womb I knew you, and before you were born I consecrated you; I appointed you a prophet to the nations" (Jeremiah 1:5).

I carried this belief with me for more than twenty years, until my views started to become more progressive in my forties. During this time, I began seeking information that did not necessarily conform to what I believed. This critical thinking allowed me to explore opinions with a more open mind and led me to this conclusion: When men start having babies, we'll have earned the right to have an opinion about what women should do with their own bodies.

I shared this with a friend of mine, who happens to be Catholic. He said he felt like my view was a cop-out, and that we not only had the right to speak out, but that we had an obligation to protect the unborn. This gets to the question of when life begins. Some, citing religious beliefs, might say that "every sperm is special" and that birth control is a sin. Others might say that "life begins at conception."

A female friend of mine opined that life begins for the baby when that baby can sustain life on its own. Until that time, she believes it's the woman's right to decide whether or not to go forward with the pregnancy. Her definition aligns with a Supreme Court case, *Planned Parenthood v. Casey* (1992), when a majority of the justices ruled that a woman has a right to abortion until fetal viability.[96]

I have enough intellectual humility to understand that I don't know when life begins. What I do know is that there are a lot of lives who need help on this planet, and as a Christian, I believe we are called to serve them. This leads me to ponder: Imagine if we spent half as much time serving those in need as we did arguing over whether a mother's rights override the rights of the unborn.

As a former conservative with libertarian leanings early in my life, I remember thinking it odd that other conservative libertarians shouted about the importance of liberty and getting the government out of people's lives—unless they wanted to use

---

96. Supreme Court Case *Roe v. Wade*, 410 U.S. 113 (1973).

government to tell others they were wrong about the beliefs that did not coincide with so-called conservative values.

Imagine if the government decided to follow the belief that "every sperm is special." What ramifications would that have for men's freedom and liberties? Some might argue that there's a fair comparison to be made for a male-dominated government deciding what's right for a woman and her reproductive rights.

I also remember during the debates about the Affordable Care Act in 2009-2010, many of my religious conservative friends argued that the government had no place getting between a patient and his doctor. But isn't that what happens when anti-abortion laws are wedged between a pregnant patient and her doctor?

I feel that many of those who oppose abortion do so with the best of intentions, believing they are trying to save a baby's life. This was how I justified my own pro-life beliefs.

At this point, let's address a few questions:

What does it mean to be pro-life?

When did the pro-life movement begin?

Why did the religious right pick up the mantle to defend the unborn? How did the Republican Party and larger conservative movement use a pro-life agenda to co-opt evangelicals into a new, powerful religious right?

Let's start with a definition of pro-life. According to Merriam-Webster, "pro-life is to oppose abortion."[97]

Sounds simple enough. However, the Cambridge Dictionary offers a more complex definition: "supporting the belief that it is immoral for a pregnant woman to have the freedom to choose to have an abortion if she does not want to have a baby.[98]

---

97. "Pro-Life," Merriam-Webster Dictionary, retrieved January 25, 2019, www.merriam-webster.com/dictionary/pro-life

98. "Pro-Life," Cambridge Dictionary, retrieved June 6, 2019, https://dictionary.cambridge.org/us/dictionary/english/pro-life

This more complex definition offers a clearer insight into the abortion issue, speaking to the beliefs, morality, and freedom.

No wonder the issue is so divisive. These terms get to the heart of what it means to be an individual with certain inalienable rights. When do people get to tell others what they can or cannot do with their bodies? More importantly, when does the government get to impose its will upon an individual exercising those rights?

Perhaps this is why in 1973 the US Supreme Court ruled 7-2 in *Roe v. Wade* that women's right to privacy under the due process clause of the Fourteenth Amendment included abortion.[99]

It's interesting to note the term "pro-life" did not exist in this context until just before this landmark Supreme Court decision. Turning back to our original source for pro-life, Merriam-Webster, we learn that the first use of the word "pro-life" was 1970. A few years prior to that, beginning in the late 1960s, many groups opposed the legalization of abortion, and the National Right to Life Committee was formed in 1968. The term "pro-life" was used in lieu of "anti-abortion" following 1973, because NRLC members believed that they were protecting life, not restricting a woman's reproductive rights.

US Catholic bishops were the first organized group to recommend a constitutional amendment banning abortion. This view was consistent with right-to-life opinions held by Catholic leaders for generations and continuing to this day, including opposition to the death penalty.[100]

While there's a long history of Catholic teachings against abortion, what's the history of other Americans concerning abortion?

"The vast majority of evangelicals said virtually nothing about

---

99. Roe v. Wade, 410 U.S. 113 (1973).

100. Jeffrey D. Schultz and Laura A. Van Assendelft, *Encyclopedia of Women in American Politics, The American Political Landscape,* Greenwood Publishing Group, 1999, p. 195.

it (*Roe v. Wade*) and many of those who did comment actually applauded the decision," according to Randall Balmer, Mandel family professor in the arts and sciences at Dartmouth College. W. Barry Garrett wrote in the *Baptist Press*, "Religious liberty, human equality, and justice are advanced by the Supreme Court abortion decision."[101]

Balmer also wrote: "In 1968, for instance, a symposium sponsored by the Christian Medical Society and *Christianity Today*, the flagship magazine of evangelicalism, refused to characterize abortion as sinful, citing 'individual health, family welfare, and social responsibility' as justifications for ending a pregnancy."[102]

Former Southern Baptist Convention president and Dallas First Baptist Church pastor W. A. Criswell opined, "I have always felt that it was only after a child was born and had a life separate from its mother that it became an individual person and it has always, therefore, seemed to me that what is best for the mother and for the future should be allowed."[103]

The Southern Baptist Convention members advocated for removing restrictions on abortion until 1980. Both the 1971 and 1974 Southern Baptist Conventions included a call "to work for legislations that will allow the possibility of abortion under (certain) conditions . . ."The convention reaffirmed this view in 1976.[104]

So, what happened in the late 1970s and early '80s to shift opinions of most evangelical Christians? In other words, why did the religious right pick up the mantle in the fight against abortion

---

101. Ziad W. Munson, *The Making of Pro-life Activists: How Social Movement Mobilization Works*, University of Chicago Press, 2008, p. 85.

102. Randall Balmer, "The Real Origins of the Religious Right," Politico, May 27, 2014, retrieved April 4, 2019, https://www.politico.com/magazine/story/2014/05/religious-right-real-origins-107133

103. Balmer, "The Real Origins."

104. Munson, *The Making of Pro-life Activists*.

rights? The answer lies in politics, more than religion.

Balmer wrote this analysis for Politico. "Evangelical leaders, at the behest of conservative activist Paul Weyrich, seized on abortion not for moral reasons, but as a rallying cry to deny President Jimmy Carter a second term. Why? Because the anti-abortion crusade was more palatable than the religious right's real motive: protecting segregated schools."[105]

The history of so-called "segregation academies" exceeds the scope of this book, but they included Jerry Falwell's Lynchburg Christian School and Bob Jones University. The issue focused on the tax-exempt status of these religious schools, which ran counter to federal law prohibiting discrimination based on race.

Randall Balmer also wrote in his article, "The Real Origins of the Religious Right," about Bob Jones University's loss of its tax-exempt status.[106]

This was a rallying cry for other religious organizations who viewed the IRS action as overreach. It was also a match made this side of heaven for the religious right and the Republican Party, which wanted to regain the White House in 1980.

Even though Ronald Reagan had signed the Therapeutic Abortion Act as governor of California, he ran as a pro-life candidate and won the election in 1980, due in part to the evangelical, anti-abortion vote. It's unclear whether those pro-life voters ever showed any disappointment in the fact that during his eight years in office he never introduced legislation to Congress regarding abortion.[107]

For nearly four decades, the marriage between conservatives and the religious right based on a mutual pro-life agenda has benefitted Republican politicians. Any benefits to women remain to be seen.

---

105. Balmer, "The Real Origins."

106. Balmer, "The Real Origins."

107. Scott Horseley, "Ronald Reagan's Legacy Clouds Tax Record," February 4, 2011, National Public Radio.

During the 2016 presidential campaign, I talked with many who were voting for Donald Trump for one reason and one reason alone: abortion. They would share their reservations about the things that Trump had said and done, but they could not bear the thought of voting for someone who would support abortion, which they believed Hillary Clinton would do. I remember talking with others in 2012, 2008, and presidential elections going back to Ronald Reagan who also had an abortion litmus test for their vote.

I, too, supported candidates based on whether they represented my values, which, until the past decade, included a pro-life stance. As I tried to learn more about other people's views about this divisive issue, I was encouraged by many pro-choice candidates who emphasized support for a woman's right to choose while also focusing on ways to reduce unintended pregnancies so that fewer women are placed in a position to make that choice. This to me seems like a rational approach to the issue, while protecting a woman's constitutional right to privacy.

While researching this issue, I stumbled across a group known as the Susan B. Anthony List, which is dedicated to "increasing the percentage of anti-abortion women in Congress and high public office," and seeks to eliminate abortion in the US.[108]

The group was founded in 1993 to counter the success of EMILY's List, which supports pro-choice candidates. Since Susan B. Anthony is a feminist history heroine, it seemed an odd match to see her name attached to an organization that many of today's feminists might consider in opposition to a feminist cause. I wonder what Susan B. Anthony would think about her name being used for an issue that today is seen as an attempt to limit the rights of women? We may never know for sure, because according to Anthony scholar Ann D. Gordon and Anthony biographer

---

108. M. Gstalter, "GOP Texas Lawmaker Reintroduces Bill to Allow Death Penalty for Women Who Have Abortions," *The Hill*, April 10, 2019.

Lynn Sherr, she "spent no time on the politics of abortion."[109]

States such as Alabama, Georgia, Louisiana, and Missouri passed so-called "heartbeat bills" that prohibit abortion once a fetal heartbeat is detected. There are at least three issues with these bills.[110] First of all, a woman may not even know she's pregnant that early, which means the bills may effectively ban all abortions. Secondly, a heart has not been formed yet at six weeks, even though a physician may detect an electrical current from the tissues that have formed at that point. And, finally, many of the bills do not allow exceptions for rape or incest. So the state is forcing a woman to carry to term a pregnancy that resulted from an unimaginably horrific crime. This seems unconscionable to me.

Just before this book was published, battle lines were being drawn in the courts over Texas's new abortion restrictions that went into effect on September 1, 2021. The law bans the procedure as soon as fetal cardiac activity can be detected. And in a heavily contentious new move, the law passes enforcement from state officials to its citizens. Ordinary people can essentially become bounty hunters, collecting thousands of dollars if they successfully sue an abortion provider or anyone who helps a woman get the procedure. Help could mean paying for it or even giving a woman a ride to the clinic. As with other early abortion bans, this one makes no exceptions for rape or incest.

Support for a woman's reproductive rights has come from many corners. For example, United Nations deputy commissioner on human rights Kate Gilmore denounced recent anti-choice laws in the US as products of "extremist hate" aimed at women and called

109. Ann D. Gordon and Lynn Sherr, "Sarah Palin Is No Susan B. Anthony," On Faith (blog), May 21, 2010, WashingtonPost.com.

110. Anna North and Catherine Kim, "The 'Heartbeat' Bills That Could Ban Almost All Abortions, Explained," May 30, 2019, retrieved June 6, 2019, https://www.vox.com/policy-and-politics/2019/4/19/18412384/abortion-heartbeat-bill-georgia-louisiana-ohio-2019

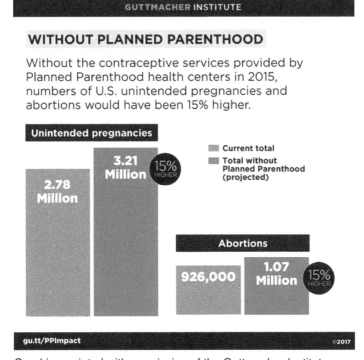

Graphic reprinted with permission of the Guttmacher Institute.

on rights advocates "to stand with the evidence and facts and in solidarity with women."[111]

The American College of Obstetricians and Gynecologists (ACOG) told reporters that "heartbeat bills" should be referred to as "six-week abortion bans," because there is no heart to produce a heartbeat that early in the pregnancy.[112]

Some anti-abortion efforts have focused on one specific organization based on quite a bit of misinformation. Doctored

---

111. Julia Conley, "Don't Call Latest Abortion Bans 'Heartbeat Bills,' Doctors Say, Warning of Medically Inaccurate Right-Wing Talking Points," June 5, 2019, retrieved June 6, 2019, https://www.commondreams.org/news/2019/06/05/dont-call-latest-abortion-bans-heartbeat-bills-doctors-say-warning-medically

112. Conley, "Don't Call Latest Abortion Bans 'Heartbeat Bills.'"

videos are often used to make outlandish claims about the services provided by Planned Parenthood.[113]

First of all, since the passage of the Hyde Amendment in 1976, federal funding for abortions is prohibited.

Secondly, abortion represents only 3 percent of all health services provided by Planned Parenthood.

Finally, Planned Parenthood has a focus on preventing unplanned pregnancies, which helps reduce the number of abortions. In 2015, it is estimated that 430,000 unintended pregnancies and 150,000 abortions were averted.[114]

---

113. Note: In the interest of full disclosure, my daughter worked at Planned Parenthood as an intern while earning her master's degree in social work at the University of Memphis.

114. Jennifer J. Frost, "Publicly Funded Contraceptive Services at US Clinics," New York: Guttmacher Institute, 2017, retrieved March 14, 2019, https://www.guttmacher.org/report/publicly-funded-contraceptive-services-us-clinics-2015

7

Women in Leadership

Over the course of my career, most of which was in the US military, I served in four commands led by women. I also worked for more than a dozen other women who were in my chain of command, including the only civilian boss I've ever had. My first ship in the Navy, a destroyer where I served from 1991-1994, had no females because of combat exclusion laws that dated back to 1948.

In the Navy, women were allowed to serve primarily ashore and aboard non-combat ships, such as supply, repair, and hospital vessels. On November 30, 1993, President Bill Clinton signed the Defense Authorization Act that repealed the prohibition against women serving aboard combat vessels.[115]

It took another twenty years before Secretary of Defense Leon Panetta repealed the ground combat exclusion policy following

---

115. Navy Live Blog, November 30, 2018, "Combat Vessels Opened to Women 25 Years Ago Today," retrieved September 8, 2019, https://navylive.dodlive. mil/2018/11/30/combat-vessels-opened-to-women-25-years-ago-today/

a unanimous recommendation by the Joint Chiefs of Staff. The commander-in-chief at the time, President Barack Obama, praised the decision: "This milestone reflects the courageous and patriotic service of women through more than two centuries of American history and the indispensable role of women in today's military."[116]

My second ship in the Navy, an aircraft carrier, was fully integrated with a female crew. I can honestly say that in hindsight there's little difference between serving male leaders and female leaders or leading male service members and female service members.

This revelation contradicts a paper this young midshipman wrote in 1987 while attending Texas Tech University on a Naval ROTC scholarship. I don't remember the details of the paper, but I do know that the thesis was that women should not serve at sea. I based my thesis on the opinions of others because, of course, I had no personal experience serving in the Navy at that time, much less any real experience in the world as an adult. Some of the objections I heard about females serving on ships included "a weaker sex" argument that they could put themselves and other sailors at risk, along with the notion that a mixed-gender crew would harm good order and discipline. One of my instructors, a Navy lieutenant, told me there were also a number of wives who were not keen on their husbands serving at sea for months at a time with members of the opposite sex.

I also remember serving as an officer escort for a distinguished visitor aboard a submarine. Prior to embarking the submarine, the distinguished visitor, who worked directly for a senior politician, asked when the Navy would allow women to serve aboard submarines. This was in 1999, and fourteen years later, females

---

116. Department of Defense, January 24, 2013, "Defense Department Expands Women's Combat Role," retrieved September 8, 2019, https://web. archive.org/web/20140412193528/http://www.defense.gov/news/newsarticle. aspx?id=119098#

finally began serving aboard submarines. I remember when this happened, we discussed how to publicize this milestone, and I was kind of torn because I wasn't sure it was really something we should be bragging about. On the one hand, it was a milestone; however, on the other hand, why did it take so long?

Fortunately, there are many women in the military who have blazed a trail as outstanding leaders. One of my favorite leadership quotes is from Rear Admiral Grace Hopper: "You manage things. You lead people." She also told a *60 Minutes* reporter during a 1983 television interview, "Leadership is a two-way street—loyalty up and loyalty down."[117]

Hopper joined the Naval Reserves in 1943 after being an associate professor of mathematics at Vassar College. She retired from the Naval Reserve with the rank of commander at the end of 1966. She was recalled to active duty in August 1967 for a six-month period that turned into an indefinite assignment. She retired from the Navy again on August 14, 1986. Owing to the breadth of her accomplishments and her naval rank, she is sometimes referred to as "Amazing Grace." The Navy named a warship in honor of Hopper, and the ship is currently stationed in Pearl Harbor, Hawaii.[118]

I never knew Hopper, but I do know Vice Admiral Nora Tyson, who was the first woman to command a Navy strike group (Carrier Strike Group Two embarked aboard the aircraft carrier *USS George H. W. Bush*). She was also the first woman to lead a numbered fleet (Third Fleet). I served with her when she was the commanding officer of Fleet Air Reconnaissance Squadron 4 in 1998. I was a lowly lieutenant at the time, but that did not matter to her. She

117. Grace Hopper quotes, retrieved May 4, 2019, https://www.azquotes.com/author/6894-Grace_Hopper

118. US Navy, Grace Hopper biography, retrieved May 20, 2019, https://www.history.navy.mil/research/histories/biographies-list/bios-h/hopper-grace.html

treated everyone with dignity and respect. When you were in her presence, you felt like you had her undivided attention. She had an innate ability to put people at ease, which inspired them to want to do their best for her and for the command. I carry many of the leadership lessons I learned from her with me today.

If there were more leaders like Tyson and Hopper today, the world would be a better place. It makes me wonder how many other leaders we've missed out on in years past because women were not allowed to serve. I also have to wonder how many female leaders we're still missing out on because of continued bias in the workplace. Yes, bias (including gender bias) still exists in the workplace.

There are, of course, examples of great leaders who happen to be female in the civilian world as well. One example is Mary Barra, the chief executive of General Motors. I'll let you read her biography on your own, but I will share this anecdote about how she changed the dress code for this international corporation with more than 150,000 employees. It's two words: "Dress Appropriately." The code was ten pages before she had it changed when she served as the head of human resources in 2009. This may seem trite, but an organization's dress code speaks to its culture, which defines success. Something as simple as a two-word dress code shows a level of trust in people's discretion, professionalism, and common sense. It also says a lot about Barra's leadership style.[119]

One study, published in *Harvard Business Review*, focused on gender behavior and inequality in the workplace. "No perceptible differences were observed in the behavior of men and women. They had the same number of contacts, spent the same amount of time with senior leaders, and allocated their time similarly. They also spend the same amount of time in online and face-to-face

---

119. Quartz at Work, "GM's Dress Code Is Only Two Words," April 3, 2018, retrieved May 10, 2019, https://qz.com/work/1242801/gms-dress-code-is-only-two-words/

conversations. Yet women weren't advancing and men were."[120]

The analysis suggested that the company's differing promotion rates were due not to behavior but to how men and women were treated, the authors said. "This indicates that arguments about changing women's behavior—to 'lean in,' for example—might miss the bigger picture: Gender inequality is due to bias, not differences in behavior."[121]

While teaching leadership courses at the undergraduate and graduate levels, I see that the issue of gender often comes up in one of two ways. Which gender makes a better boss, and which one would you rather follow?

I don't have any empirical evidence to share, but I can offer anecdotal evidence that most of my female students report that they would prefer to work for a man and most of my male students report that they have no preference.

This is not a scientific study, so we can't make too many conclusions, but I think it's interesting to note that, at least for a majority of my students, there are preferences for male leaders by females, but this does not seem to be the case for my male students. Of course, it may be that the men are too politically sensitive to admit they have a preference; however, follow-up discussions with some of these students, as well as fellow military colleagues, tend to reveal the same results.

My own limited findings seem to follow the pattern offered by Tomas Chamorro-Premuzic, who wrote this in *Harvard Business Review*: "So long as we continue to associate leadership with masculine features, we can expect female leaders to be evaluated more negatively even when their performance is higher than that

---

120. *Harvard Business Review*, "What Research Tells Us About How Women Are Treated at Work," December 27, 2017, retrieved February 20, 2019, https://hbr.org/2017/12/what-research-tells-us-about-how-women-are-treated-at-work

121. *Harvard Business Review*, "What Research Tells Us."

of their male counterparts, and even when those who evaluate them are women."[122]

Premuzic also found, "While overall gender differences in leadership effectiveness are generally nonexistent, meta-analytic studies show that men tend to perform better when the focus is on managing tasks, while women tend to perform better when the focus is on managing people, which includes attending to people's attitudes, values, and motivation. (These differences are predominantly attributable to cultural constructs, not biological differences.)"[123]

As more women break invisible barriers, one would assume that firsts would become less frequent; however, it seems that barely a month goes by before another female first makes the news. I love reading these stories, and I'm grateful that progress is being made in so many non-traditional areas, but I look forward to the day when these stories don't make news because they are such a common occurrence.

One personal story that comes to mind is the first-ever female "missing man" formation to honor US Navy Captain Rosemary Mariner, one of the first women to fly a naval aircraft. After her death on January 24, 2019, the Navy wanted to fly over her hometown of Maynardville, Tennessee, during the funeral on February 2. The idea was to have the "missing man" formation flown by all females. During the planning process, a male public affairs officer asked if it was appropriate to refer to the formation as a "missing man" formation, since the intent was to honor a pioneering female with all female aviators. Personally, I thought it was a reasonable question to ask, but two senior female commanders pounced on

122. *Harvard Business Review*, "As Long As We Associate Leadership with Masculinity, Women Will Be Overlooked," March 8, 2019, retrieved May 30, 2019, https://hbr.org/2019/03/as-long-as-we-associate-leadership-with-masculinity-women-will-be-overlooked

123. *Harvard Business Review*, "As Long As We Associate."

him, making it clear that the "missing man" formation was a time-honored tradition and that the name should not be changed. To me, it spoke to the sensitivities surrounding naming conventions that for most of history were dominated by men.

Another example was the first all-female spacewalk scheduled for March 2019, featuring Anne McClain and Christina Koch. The two astronauts would have been supported on the ground by flight director Mary Lawrence and flight control team member Kristen Facciol. Unfortunately, the history-making spacewalk did not happen because there was a mix-up on what size spacesuit McClain could wear, which meant that she had to be replaced by one of her male colleagues. The mission still took place, but it did not feature an all-female spacewalk. While it was an embarrassment to NASA, from my perspective it's one more example of a first that I hope will one day be routine. The first all-female spacewalk did happen later that year, when astronauts Christina Koch and Jessica Meir performed that milestone in October 2019.

I'm a big fan of research, especially objective research based on reputable polling. Gallup is one of my favorite sources because of their longstanding dedication to helping leaders solve problems. Gallup asked, "Who makes a better boss? Him or her." Their response, "It's a trick question: Gender doesn't matter. Talent does." I believe that most people with experience serving with both male and female leadership could honestly answer that talent is much more important than gender. In fact, there are scores of other leadership qualities that are more important in the workplace, yet gender is still a common quality that is misunderstood as it relates to leadership.[124]

Gender is still a contributing factor in how effective women are perceived and paid for their leadership in the workplace. According

---

124. Gallup, "Who Makes a Better Boss, Him or Her?" January 8, 2018, retrieved February 4, 2109, https://www.gallup.com/workplace/236234/makes-better-boss.aspx?utm_source=alert&utm_medium=email&utm_content=morelink&utm_campaign=syndication

to a 2018 study published by the University of Chicago, how much a woman makes and how much work she gets depends on the level of sexism in the state where she was born. "Sexism experienced during formative years stays with girls into adulthood, and this sexism can have a significant impact on a woman's wages and labor market participation," according to the study's authors.[125]

Another benchmark polling organization I use to better understand views on social issues is the Pew Research Center, which released a series of reports about American views on gender equality, gender differences, and gender identity. As expected, opinions differed based on one's gender and party affiliation.

About half of Americans say granting women the right to vote has been the most important milestone in advancing the position of women in the country, authors Juliana Menasce Horowitz and Ruth Igielnik wrote in a 2020 report on the Pew survey. Despite seeing some progress, most adults say the country hasn't gone far enough when it comes to giving women equal rights with men.

Those who think there still is work to do target various issues as major obstacles:[126]

• 77 percent point to sexual harassment.

• 67 percent point to women not having the same legal rights as men.

• 66 percent point to different societal expectations for women.

• 64 percent point to not enough women in positions of power.

---

125. Kerwin Kofi Charles, Jonathan Guryan, and Jessica Pan, "The Effects of Sexism on American Women: The Role of Norms vs. Discrimination," August 17, 2018, University of Chicago, Becker Friedman Institute, https://bfi.uchicago.edu/Charles-WP-201856

126. Juliana Menasce Horowitz and Ruth Igielnik, "A Century after Women Gained the Right to Vote, Majority of Americans See Work to Do on Gender Equality," excerpts from July 7, 2020, Pew Research Center, https://www. pewresearch.org/social-trends/2020/07/07/a-century-after-women-gained-the-right-to-vote-majority-of-americans-see-work-to-do-on-gender-equality

Women are more likely to see each of these as a major obstacle.

"Many of those who say it is important for men and women to have equal rights point to aspects of the workplace when asked about what gender equality would look like," the report said. "Fully 45 percent volunteer that a society where women have equal rights with men would include equal pay. An additional 19 percent say there would be no discrimination in hiring, promotion or educational opportunities. About one in ten say women would be more equally represented in business or political leadership."[127]

Other key findings:[128]

• Democratic women, those with a bachelor's degree or more education, and women younger than fifty are among the most likely to say they've benefitted personally from feminism.

• Opinions vary along party lines. About 76 percent of Democrats say the country hasn't gone far enough when it comes to giving women equal rights with men, while 19 percent say it's been about right and 4 percent say the country has gone too far. Among Republicans, a third say the country hasn't made enough progress, while 48 percent say it's been about right and 17 percent say the country has gone too far in giving women equal rights with men.

• What has been the most important milestone for women? More Americans point to woman suffrage than other achievements. About 49 percent point to the right to vote; 29 percent cite the passage of the Equal Pay Act, while smaller shares point to the passage of the Family and Medical Leave Act (12 percent) or the availability of the birth control pill (8 percent) as the most important milestone.

• Most Americans favor adding the Equal Rights Amendment to the US Constitution, even as many don't think this would make much difference for women's rights.

---

127. Horowitz and Igielnik, "A Century after."

128. Horowitz and Igielnik, "A Century after."

Growing share of Americans say the country has not gone far enough in giving women equal rights with men

% saying, when it comes to giving women equal rights with men, they think our country has ...

Total	Not gone far enough	Gone too far	Been about right
March 2020	57	10	32
Aug/Sept 2017	50	10	39
Men			
March 2020	49	12	37
Aug/Sept 2017	42	13	44
Women			
March 2020	64	8	27
Aug/Sept 2017	57	8	33
Republicans and Republican leaners			
March 2020	33	17	48
Aug/Sept 2017	26	18	54
Democrats and Democratic leaners			
March 2020	76	4	19
Aug/Sept 2017	69	4	26

Note: Share of respondents who didn't offer an answer not shown. In 2017, the question was asked about "the country." In 2020, the question wording was changed to "our country."
Source: Survey of U.S. adults conducted March 18-April 1, 2020.
"A Century After Women Gained the Right To Vote, Majority of Americans See Work To Do on Gender Equality"

PEW RESEARCH CENTER

Graphic reprinted with permission

About eight in ten adults (78 percent)—including majorities of men and women and Republicans and Democrats alike—say they at least somewhat favor adopting the ERA. When asked about the impact it might have, 44 percent say it would advance women's rights, 5 percent say this would be a setback for women's rights, and 49 percent say it would not make much of a difference.

8

Where Do We Go from Here?

I borrowed the title of this conclusion from Dr. Martin Luther King Jr., a person I wrote about in my previous book, *I Have a Dream: A Report Card Fifty Years After Dr. King's Assassination.* I chose this title because, much like civil rights for Blacks, we've made progress for the rights of women, but we still have a long way to go.

What steps could, and should, we take, if we truly care about our mothers, daughters, sisters, and all of us who are influenced by the treatment of those who make up half our population and gave birth to all of it?

There are moral and philosophical reasons to ensure equal rights for all, of course. There are also practical reasons why we should all want to fight for the rights of women.

"The US economy will not operate at its full potential unless government and employers remove impediments to full participation by women in the labor market," according to a Brookings Institute report. "The failure to address structural problems in labor markets, tax, and employment policy that women face does more than hold back their careers and aspirations for a better life. In fact, barriers to participation by women also act as brakes on the national economy, stifling the economy's ability to grow. The lives and fortunes of women in the workplace affect us all."[129]

One item that transcends equal rights for women is equal pay. The American Association of University Women conducted a study titled "The Simple Truth About the Gender Pay Gap." They concluded that a woman working full time is paid 80 percent of what a man is paid.[130]

The researchers also found that education may increase a woman's overall earnings potential, but it does not remove the gap between the earnings of men and women. At the current rate of change, the study says, the gender pay gap in the United States would not close until 2119![131]

"Your organization won't be able to compete for exceptional talent until you implement major structural and policy changes that transform your culture into one that is high-performing and inclusive, respectful and caring," according to Jane Miller, Gallup's chief operating officer.[132]

To create change quickly and bring more women into leadership positions, she recommends recruiting and developing women,

---

129. Diane Whitmore Schanzenbach and Ryan Nunn, "The 51%: Driving Growth Through Women's Economic Participation," Brookings, October 9, 2017, retrieved July 30, 2019, https://www.brookings.edu/multi-chapter-report/the-51-percent-driving-growth-through-womens-economic-participation/

130. DJ Vagins, "The Simple Truth About the Gender Pay Gap," The American Association of University Women, retrieved August 1, 2019, https://www.aauw.org/research/the-simple-truth-about-the-gender-pay-gap/

131. Vagins, "The Simple Truth."

132. Jane Miller, "No More Excuses. Recruit and Develop Women Leaders," Gallup Blog, March 8, 2019, retrieved August 4, 2019, https://news.gallup.com/opinion/gallup/247184/no-excuses-recruit-develop-women-leaders.aspx

while retaining them with a culture that meets their needs.

So, there are objective, measurable economic reasons for women's equality. More importantly, it's the right thing to do—for everyone.

Men and women benefit when we treat everyone with dignity and respect, and this can't happen by simply pretending that inequality does not exist. It can't happen if good men do nothing. And, in this case, I am using Edmund Burke's specific male gender to make the point that we men have a role to play in this important social issue.[133]

If you're a man ready to make a difference, here are some actions to consider, based on an article in *Harvard Business Review*.[134]

• **First, just listen.**

Listening to women's voices in a way that inspires trust and respect is a fundamental relationship promise you must make, and then keep, with women who invite you to participate around equity.

• **Respect the space.**

Tread respectfully into these areas (women's conferences and other meetings) and before you utter a word, revisit the recommendation above.

• **Remember, it's not about you.**

Ask women how you can amplify, not usurp, existing gender parity efforts. A large dose of gender humility will help here.

• **Get comfortable being uncomfortable.**

Developing psychological standing requires a commitment to learning and advocating for gender equity.

• **Engage in supportive partnerships with women.**

---

133. Edmund Burke, "The only thing necessary for the triumph of evil is for good men to do nothing," as quoted in a 1770 letter addressed to Thomas Mercer.

134. W. Brad Johnson and David G. Smith, "How Men Can Become Better Allies to Women," *Harvard Business Review*, October 12, 2018, retrieved July 1, 2019, https://hbr.org/2018/10/how-men-can-become-better-allies-to-women

The best cross-gender ally relationships are reciprocal and mutually growth-enhancing.
• **Remember the two parts to allyship.**
Keep in mind that committing to express as little sexism as possible is the easy part of allyship.

* * *

Here are some ideas on priorities from women, who know a lot more about this issue than I, or any other man, ever will.[135]
• **Marillyn Hewson, CEO, Lockheed Martin:** "One big thing that will matter for women is economic empowerment. Opening the doors of opportunity for women is key to equality for women, to economic growth and to business success."
• **Mary Barra, CEO, GM:** "One big thing that will matter to women is equal pay. I think companies have a big role to play in making this happen. And we all need to realize that not only is it a moral issue, but it is a business issue."
• **Stacey Stewart, president, March of Dimes:** "We want every woman to be able to afford her health care so that when she is ready to become a mom, she and her baby, no matter what they look like or where they live, can be as healthy as they can be."
• **Bellamy Young, actress and advocate:** "One big thing that will matter to women is the fight against harassment at work . . . so that we can give of our brains and our hearts and our passions without restraint or fear."

* * *

Although there are many organizations focused on feminism, I offer the following for the reader's consideration. I include descriptions from and links to their websites:
9to5: Women Working for Equal Pay, Power, and Participation
"9to5 members have been on the frontlines, working for economic

---

135. "Women Give Their 1 Big Thing," Axios, retrieved April 8, 2019, https://www.axios.com/newsletters/axios-am-46dd03c5-0914-4915-93d7-05f6057caeca.html

security for all women—particularly women of color—for the past 45 years. We still have many barriers to overcome before we achieve our vision—*full economic equality*." https://9to5.org

Click! The Ongoing Feminist Revolution

"In the 1970s that word (Click!) signaled the moment when a woman awakened to the powerful ideas of contemporary feminism. Today 'click' usually refers to a computer keystroke that connects women (and men) to powerful ideas on the Internet. We aim to bridge the gap between those two clicks by offering an exhibit that highlights the achievements of women from the 1940s to the present. This exhibit explores the power and complexity of gender consciousness in modern American life." https://www.cliohistory.org/click

Christian Feminism Today

"CFT is a community faithful to Christ's example, pursuing social justice and offering radical welcome to all. We believe answers to hard questions can be found through careful feminist examination of the Bible. We value diverse religious experiences." https://eewc.com/about/

Feminist Majority Foundation

"The name Feminist Majority Foundation is a consciousness-raiser, inspired by a Newsweek/Gallup public opinion poll that showed the majority of women (56%) in the United States self-identified as feminists. Most polls since then reveal that this majority continues with over two-thirds of young women self-identifying as feminists. Most men, especially young men, view themselves as supporters of the women's rights movement. The Feminist Majority Foundation, which was founded in 1987, is a cutting-edge organization dedicated to women's equality, reproductive health, and non-violence. In all spheres, FMF utilizes research and action to empower women economically, socially, and politically. Our organization believes that feminists—both women and men, girls and boys—are the majority, but this majority must be empowered." http://www.feminist.org

He for She

Invites men—and people of all genders—to stand in solidarity with women to create a bold, visible, and united force for gender equality. http://www.heforshe.org/en

League of Women Voters

"We envision a democracy where every person has the desire, the right, the knowledge, and the confidence to participate. We believe in the power of women to create a more perfect democracy. The League is proud to be nonpartisan, neither supporting nor opposing candidates or political parties at any level of government, but always working on vital issues of concern to members and the public." https://www.lwv.org

Legal Momentum

"Legal Momentum believes that every woman and girl is entitled to a safe space at home, at school, and at work, and should have an equal voice in society. Legal Momentum is working to make this ideal a reality. Legal Momentum's mission is to ensure economic and personal security for all women and girls by advancing equity in education, the workplace, and the courts. We provide an expert legal voice to seek justice for women." https://www.legalmomentum.org

National Women's History Alliance

"The National Women's History Alliance, formerly the National Women's History Project, is a leader in promoting Women's History and is committed to the goals of education, empowerment, equality, and inclusion." https://nationalwomenshistoryalliance.org

National Organization for Men Against Sexism

This activist organization of men and women supports positive changes for men. "NOMAS advocates a perspective that is pro-feminist, gay affirmative, anti-racist, dedicated to enhancing men's lives, and committed to justice on a broad range of social issues including class, age, religion, and physical abilities. As an organization for changing men, we strongly support the continuing struggle of women for full equality. We affirm that working to make this nation's ideals of equality substantive is the finest expression of what it means to be men." http://nomas.org

National Organization for Women

"As the grassroots arm of the women's movement, the National Organization for Women is dedicated to its multi-issue and multi-strategy approach to women's rights, and is the largest organization of feminist grassroots activists in the United States. NOW has hundreds of chapters and hundreds of thousands of members and activists in all 50 states and the District of Columbia. Since our founding in 1966, NOW's purpose is to take action through intersectional grassroots activism to promote feminist ideals, lead societal change, eliminate discrimination, and achieve and protect the equal rights of all women and girls in all aspects of social, political, and economic life." https://now.org

National Partnership for Women and Families

"We believe that actions speak louder than words. And for four decades, we have fought for every major policy advance that has helped women and families. Founded in 1971 as the Women's Legal Defense Fund, the National Partnership for Women & Families is a nonprofit, nonpartisan 501(c)(3) organization located in Washington, DC. Today, we promote fairness in the workplace; reproductive health and rights; access to quality, affordable health care; and policies that help women and men meet the dual demands of work and family." http://www.nationalpartnership.org

Veteran Feminists of America Inc.

"The purpose of Veteran Feminists of America Inc. is to honor, record, and preserve the history of the accomplishments of women and men active in the feminist movement, to educate the public on the importance of the changes brought about by the women's movement, and to preserve the movement's history for future generations. VFA Inc. is a nonprofit organization for supporters and veterans of the Second Wave of the feminist revolution. It is the foremost national source of information about the modern women's movement for journalists, historians, archivists, and writers." http://www.veteranfeministsofamerica.org

WEDO

"As a global women's advocacy organization, WEDO envisions a just world that promotes and protects human rights, gender equality, and the integrity of the environment. To contribute toward its vision for the world, WEDO's mission is to ensure that women's rights; social, economic and environmental justice; and sustainable development principles—as well as the linkages between them—are at the heart of global and national policies, programs, and practices." https://wedo.org

Women Employed

For more than forty-five years, Women Employed has mobilized "people and organizations to expand educational and employment opportunities for America's working women. We're very proud of the tremendous advances so many women have made over the past four decades. Yet millions of women are still trapped in low-paying jobs. Our vision: All women are treated fairly in the workplace, are able to attain the skills they need for the jobs they want, and are respected for the work they do." https://womenemployed.org

Join the conversation
Do you know of organizations that should be added to this list?
Feel free to share your ideas or simply join the discussion at OneMansFeminism.org.

Alvin Plexico, PhD
Commander, US Navy (Retired)

As a lifelong learner, Dr. Plexico enjoys teaching graduate and undergraduate courses in communication, crisis management, ethics, leadership, management, organizational behavior, organizational development and change, public speaking, qualitative research, social media, and strategy.

A twenty-two-year Navy career included service as a Pentagon press officer, a spokesperson for the US Pacific Fleet, and director of communication of the Center for Career Development.

He earned a bachelor's degree in business management, a master's degree in communication, and a doctor of philosophy degree in organizational leadership.

Alvin and Lucinda, his wife of thirty-three years, live near Memphis, Tennessee. Their daughter, Savannah, serves others as a social worker. Their daughter, Shiloh, serves in the Air Force.

Alvin enjoys reading, running, and following Texas Rangers baseball. In an attempt to diversify his physical activities, he races in triathlons, with the ultimate goal of completing an Ironman.

Alvin's previous books include *I Have a Dream: A Report Card 50 Years After Dr. King's Assassination* and *Lessons From Our Grandparents: An Oral History.*

Dr. Plexico enjoys connecting with other lifelong learners through his blog at www.drplexico.com.

CPSIA information can be obtained
at www.ICGtesting.com
Printed in the USA
LVHW071921041221
705143LV00005B/13